de Gruyter Studies in Organization 15

Boards of Directors Under Public Ownership

de Gruyter Studies in Organization

An international series by internationally known authors presenting current fields of research in organization.

Organizing and organizations are substantial pre-requisites for the viability and future developments of society. Their study and comprehension are indispensable to the quality of human life. Therefore, the series aims to:

– offer to the specialist work material in form of the most important and current problems, methods and results;
– give interested readers access to different subject areas;
– provide aids for decisions on contemporary problems and stimulate ideas.

The series will include monographs, collections of contributed papers, and handbooks.

Miriam Dornstein

Boards of Directors
Under Public Ownership:
a Comparative Perspective

Walter de Gruyter · Berlin · New York 1988

Dr. *Miriam Dornstein*
University of Haifa
Mount Carmel
Haifa 31999
Israel

HD
62.35
D67
1988

Library of Congress Cataloging in Publication Data

> Dornstein, Miriam, 1035
> Boards of directors under public ownership : a comparative perspective /
> Miriam Dornstein.
> p. cm. — (De Gruyter studies in organization : 15)
> Bibliography: p.
> Includes index.
> ISBN 0–89925–496–9 :
> 1. Corporations. Government—Management. 2. Government business
> enterprises—Management. 3. Directors of corporations. I. Title.
> II. Series.
> HD62.35.D67 1988   88–29750
> 350.009'2—dc19   CIP

Deutsche Bibliothek Cataloging in Publication Data

> **Dornstein, Miriam:**
> Boards of directors under public ownership: a comparative perspective /
> Miriam Dornstein. – Berlin ; New York : de Gruyter, 1988
> (De Gruyter studies in organization ; 15)
> ISBN 3-11-011740-1
> NE: GT

♾ Printed on acid free paper.

Typesetting: Wagner GmbH, Nördlingen. – Printing: Gerike GmbH, Berlin. – Binding:
Lüderitz & Bauer, GmbH, Berlin. – Cover Design: Hansbernd Lindemann, Berlin. –
Printed in Germany.

Acknowledgements

The idea of the present research was sparked by the impressions gained during the time I served as the chief economic adviser of a public enterprise. I was then a close witness of the many complications in decision making arising from the "dual nature" of the enterprise. When at a later stage I became a "detached" academic I began to entertain the idea of investigating some of the issues relating to this problem from the perspective of those most deeply involved in it – the top-level leadership. Those with whom I shared my thoughts liked the idea but had severe doubts about its feasibility. Now, I am glad to be able to express my thanks first to those who held in their hands the key to the project's success: the Board Chairmen, the Board Members and the Chief Executives who agreed to cooperate and dedicate some of their time to the investigation.

There are many others whose contributions were crucial and to whom I am grateful: To Bilha Mannheim who witnessed my first steps and, as my Ph. D. instructor, faithfully accompanied me through all the stages of the Israeli phase. Her suggestions and comments were of great value to me.

To David Hickson and Peter Olsen for their most useful comments on an earlier version of this book.

David Hickson's assistance and his good advice during my stay in Britain and his encouragement during the last phases of writing this book were invaluable. Indeed, I doubt if without his warm interest and his continuous encouragement the project would have reached this stage.

To the Research Authority at Haifa University and the British Council who funded the field research, and to the Management Centre at the Bradford University who served as my host during the British phase of the research.

To my research assistants Amir Helman, Moshe Landau and Sarah Godelnik who helped with the data collection.

Thanks are also due to the Journal of Behavioral Economics for allowing me to use, in Chapter 5, some materials of mine published in the 1976 issue, and to the Journal of Occupational Psychology for allowing me to use, in Chapter 8, some materials published in the 1977 issue.

The responsibility for the work as it is, is wholly mine: I am responsible

for the analytical approach chosen, the ideas expressed and data presented. Whatever faults one can find in all these – they are all mine.

Haifa, September 1988   *Miriam Dornstein*

Contents

List of Tables and Figures

Tables

x

Figures

Introduction

Since the pioneering work of Berle and Means (1932), on the separation of ownership and control in the modern corporation, the limelight has gradually turned to the professional managers: it is their behavior, attitudes, and motives that are assumed to be the cornerstone in revealing the operational objectives of the large modern corporation.

Theories of managerial enterprise, explicitly or tacitly accepting the dominant role of managers, have focused on the formulation of managerial objectives and their motivational determinants. Three major approaches are discernible. One emphasizes self-interest as the dominant motivating force guiding the actions of managers. Maximization of personal remuneration, desire for power, status and prestige, need for personal security, and so forth, are seen as the major forces guiding managerial actions and decisions. This view has been readily adopted by economists who have then proceeded to examine theoretically and empirically the implications of these types of "motives" for the conduct of the corporation; there is wide agreement that when translated into operational objectives the result is the pursuit of growth – profit becoming a constraint instead of being a major aim (e.g., Baumol 1959; Marris 1964; Williamson 1967).

As a major motivating force of managers another stream of writers stress what using Herriman Maurer's phrase (1955) may be described as "the responsible corporation" (e.g., Berle 1955; Drucker 1961; Knauth 1948). The principal argument here is that management has become a profession and professional managers tend to regard themselves as being socially responsible for the benefit of virtually all those who come into contact with the corporation, and for the benefit of society at large; "in the typical case ... [they] subordinate the old-fashioned hunt for profits to a variety of other, quantitatively less precise but qualitatively more worthy objectives" (Baran and Sweezy 1968: 138).

Many writers, however, regard corporate responsibility with deep skepticism (e.g., Kempner 1974: 155–156; Child 1969: 227, 377–378). Their approach is essentially behavioral. A basic argument often voiced by those taking this approach is that since profitability provides the most suitable measure of performance, and since, therefore, managers tend to be assessed largely on the basis of their economic performance – it is quite unlikely that they would be motivated by social responsibility; rather, they would tend to strive for achievement in regard to the criterion which is used to assess their performance, i.e., profit (e.g., Nichols 1969: 124–125; Kempner 1974: 155–156). Another important argument concerns the constraints within which managers in a competitive economy operate. The argument is that in a free-enterprise economy, the diversion of resources from profits to other objectives endangers the very existence of the corporation. Finally, a no less persuasive argument is that alternative objectives to that of profitability have not yet been formulated and that the institutional means for the implementation of such objectives do not yet exist (e.g., Davis and Bloomstrom 1975: 35).

While the battleground between theories of managerial motivation is largely academic insofar as private enterprise is concerned, this is not the case regarding public enterprise. Here, the conceptions concerning managerial motivation exert – implicitly or explicitly – a major influence on the theory and practice regarding the top-level managerial organization of these enterprises.

The major question occupying the minds of those concerned with the conduct of public enterprise is how best to achieve and reconcile their "dual obligation: on the one hand to be mindful of the public interest and on the other to operate as efficient commercial bodies" (Robson 1967/68: 104). Thus, while social responsibility in private enterprise is viewed by some to exist "by default" (perhaps as an unintended consequence of separating ownership from control, while, conversely, others see it as desirable but hardly attainable in practice), it is an officially recognized and fully institutionalized goal in state-owned corporations. It is given equal status to commercial efficiency and is thereby made its constant rival. The issue of ownership and control, the nature of relationships between government and the managements of the enterprises, occupies a central place in the debates about what the best solutions are. The basic questions here are:

1. Should the conduct of these corporations be put into the hands of autonomous managements, or not?
2. What should be the responsibilities of the managements? Could an autonomous management be entrusted with the custody of the "public interest", and to what extent? Or, should matters relating to the public interest be left in the hands of government only?

3. Would the managerial autonomy necessary for the achievement of commercial efficiency not be misused by managers to further their selfish goals and interests?
4. Would a management made responsible for commercial efficiency only not act in ways which contradict the public interest?
5. Would a management charged with the responsibility for both commercial efficiency and the public interest be able, at all, to orientate itself equally to both, and how?

The various opinions regarding managerial organization in public enterprise are reflected in a series of normative models concerning the functions and structure of the Board of Directors.

A closer examination of these models reveals that the rather wide discrepancies between them are largely traceable to divergent premises regarding the motivations, orientations, role perceptions, and resultant behaviors of the prospective managers.

Since little systematic empirical evidence exists to support the various theories of managerial motivation (e.g., Nichols 1969: 160 et passim), and even less so with regard to public enterprise, each of the various models can claim validity.

The research which is the subject of this book was guided by the belief that an investigation focusing on the orientations and role perceptions of directors and chief executives in the public enterprise sector could provide some of the empirical evidence needed to reduce the speculative element, revolving around managerial motivation, in the controversy about the structure and functions of the board of directors in public enterprise. Chapter 2 exposes the core elements of the debate through a schematic presentation of the various normative models concerning the functions and structure of the board of directors in public enterprise, and through an examination of the major underlying premises on which these models rest. This examination is followed by a formulation of the major research questions that led to the present investigation.

Chapter 3 is intended to deepen the insight into the issues involved and add a dimension of concreteness to the theoretical analysis given in Chapter 2: It brings into orbit some existing patterns that closely resemble some of the models discussed in Chapter 2, and highlights the problems associated with each of them as they are reflected in the relevant literature.

Analysis of the basic premises underlying the theory of the board of directors in public enterprise reveals that a major point of disagreement relates to the ability of managers in public enterprise to identify with, orient themselves toward, and be guided by the public interest. Indeed, here we have an interesting paradox. While some students of private enterprise regard social responsibility as a somewhat "deviant" behavior of managers, an unintended, but unavoidable, result of the professionalization of management, many students of public enterprise are doubtful and skeptical about the ability of its management to show the necessary and desired social responsibility, and question the wisdom of demanding such responsibility from it. While the contention that private business is dominated by a socially responsible management has been used by some to underpin the argument that public ownership is no longer a prerequisite of a publicly controlled economy (e.g., Crosland 1956), some students of public enterprise are still plagued by the question of whether the custody of the public interest could be safely placed in the hands of their managements. Obviously, such a paradox can only exist where theory is relatively free from the reins of empirical knowledge. Thus, a major purpose of our inquiry was to find out what are – in practice – the goal orientations of managers in public enterprise. What are their conceptions concerning the objectives of the corporations for which they are responsible? How far do they identify with and show concern for the two official objectives of public enterprise: commercial efficiency and the public interest? Insofar as orientations vary, what are the contingencies affecting the varying orientations? Our findings regarding these questions are reported in Chapter 5.

A second issue of debate, closely interwoven with the first, concerns the question of governmental control. The difficulty stems from what is known as the "autonomy versus control dilemma." The widely agreed upon assumption is that "too much" control could be detrimental to the achievement of commercial efficiency; ministerial intervention in the conduct of the corporation is shunned by its management, and has an adverse effect on managerial motivation and initiative. Being largely impressionistic, this assumption provides little guidance for the regulation of relationships between the corporation and government, since little is known about the actual reactions of management toward the various facets of governmental control. The major questions are: What are the views of the leadership in public enterprise toward the use of the corporation for the implementation of various short- and long-term socioeconomic policies? What are the feelings generated by ministerial control and intervention? Do those responsible for the public corporation (as some maintain) indeed feel powerless and unable to exercise initiative, as a result of constraints imposed on them by public control? Chapter 6 reports our findings regarding these questions.

Normative models of organization deal with role prescriptions, the roles which the various participants *ought* to fulfill. Prescribed patterns, however, can only survive if sustained by the appropriate role perceptions of the role incumbents and they tend to break down in the face of significant divergencies in these perceptions. Thus, a third major line of inquiry was to clarify how those actually engaged in the management of public enterprise view their own and their partners' roles. What are their views concerning the function of the board of directors? How do full-time board members, bearing executive responsibility, and part-time members, without such responsibility, perceive their roles on the board? What are their mutual expectations of each other? How well do the actual workings of the board fit the prescribed and expected patterns? The findings regarding these questions are reported in Chapter 7.

While the theory of the board of directors in public enterprise shows many divisions of opinion, there are some dominant concerns that are shared by all and that exert a no less profound impact on the theory than those issues which are in dispute. Thus, there is widespread awareness that the active management in public enterprise acts under conditions that differ sharply in some respects from those faced by the active management in the private sector. Prominent among these conditions are the multiplicity of goals characteristic of the public enterprise, the need for close public control over its decision-making process, and the pressures and cross-pressures from various interest groups facing it. There is great concern that these conditions might adversely affect the active management and impair its ability to fulfill its role adequately. Thus, there is concern that the active management might lose its sense of direction in the face of the multiple and often conflicting goals imposed on the enterprise; there is concern that its sense of self-direction and responsibility may be impaired by the constraints imposed by the controlling agencies on its freedom of decision; and there is concern that the pressures and cross-pressures from various interest groups will result in severe role-stress among them. These concerns are translated into a series of research questions that are dealt with in Chapter 8.

Chapters 5 to 8 are mainly descriptive and deal only very little with the interpretation of the findings. This task is taken up in Chapter 9, where the various findings are drawn together and discussed in light of relevant organizational theories. Then they are confronted with the prevalent theories of the board of directors in public enterprise, as discussed in Chapter 2.

In Chapter 10 the conclusions derived from the findings of the present research are further integrated into a set of proposed models for the board of directors in public enterprise. The models are derived from a conceptual framework that proposes the adoption of a contingency approach to the board of directors in public enterprise. The basic argument put forth is that different contingencies call for different structural solutions: The models proposed exemplify some such basic solutions. The contingency perspective is then applied for re-evaluating the existing patterns described in Chapter 3. The re-evaluation casts a different light on these patterns than that reflected in the prevalent literature and leads to a different view of the problems associated with them.

A schematic description of the settings chosen for the investigation is given in Chapter 4, which also describes the samples chosen for the investigation and outlines the general methodology of the research.

Chapter 1 provides a description of the general background of our research. It describes the wider context of the public enterprise sector in mixed economies and puts the questions raised into the more general perspective of the control of public enterprises in a free-market economy.

Chapter One
Problems of Public Ownership

Public ownership of industries and services in the free-market economies has come into being out of a variety of specific needs and the reasons for their establishment are manifold (e.g., Floyd 1984; Aharoni 1986). Only in a few cases, for example, the postwar nationalizations in Great Britain and France, was the establishment of public enterprises guided by a definite political theory accompanied by a definite set of legislative and administrative measures. Nowadays, the public enterprise is a well-entrenched phenomenon in most mixed economies. Indeed, the common usage of the term "mixed economies" exemplifies this well. A recent statistical study overviewing, on a worldwide basis, the public-enterprise sector in mixed economies (Short 1984) indicates that in the mid-1970s public enterprise accounted for an average of 16.5% capital formation for over 70 countries excluding the USA, and 9.5% of the GDP (gross domestic product) for 50 countries, also excluding the USA. Moreover, the same study indicates that "these high averages are not simply a reflection of large public-enterprise sectors in a few countries: public enterprises are now of major quantitative importance in most of the countries" (Short 1984: 115). A further analysis in the above study shows that the full weight of the public-enterprise sector in most of the economies is even greater than shown by the above global statistics. This is due to the combined effect of a number of factors. First, in most countries, the major part, and often almost the whole of the public utilities – electricity, gas, water, and the communications and nonroad transport industries – are publicly owned. Second, in many countries, and especially the developing countries public enterprise is prominent in natural resource industries and in heavy industries which are regarded to be of key economic importance because of their forward links with other parts of the economy or because of their links with international trade (Short 1984: 134–135). Third, many public enterprises are very large in absolute terms which means that they "can exert considerable economic power" (Short 1984: 144).

From a longer range perspective, it seems that public enterprise "is here to stay," at least for the foreseeable future. While over time there have been fluctuations in the share of public enterprise in various mixed economies, the overall trend has been one of growth. In the 1980s a climate favoring denationalization or privatization has spread over many of the developed countries, such as the United Kingdom, Canada, West Germany, France, Italy, and Japan and some of the developing countries such as Turkey, India, Brazil, and South Korea. Yet the growth trend continues in most of the developing countries (Short 1984). Even where a strong drive for denationalization and privatization prevails, like in Britain, many obstacles for its implementation present themselves (Redwood and Hatch 1982; Heald 1984; Aharoni 1986) and it is doubtful whether such a drive will result in a wholesale liquidation of the public enterprise sector. Moreover, some of the manifold reasons for the establishment of public enterprise are so well-rooted and persistent that they are unlikely to be touched much by the prevalence of any particular climate; for an extensive review of these reasons, see Aharoni (1986) and Floyd (1984).

Notwithstanding the fact that public enterprise has been with us for a relatively long time (e.g., Aharoni 1986: Chap. 3) and occupies an important place in most mixed economies, none has yet achieved a really satisfactory solution for an ever-puzzling and persistent problem which presents itself: How is the public enterprise to be effectively controlled in order to ensure implementation of its goals and efficient use of its (often vast) resources? As Sir Peter Parker put it recently: "The control and accountability of public enterprise is a theme that has foxed a generation" (Redwood and Hatch 1982: iv). While the problem of control is not unique to public enterprise, it is much more complicated than in private enterprise for several reasons (e.g., Vernon and Aharoni 1981: 7–22). First, state-owned enterprises are usually created with many different purposes in mind. These may be both financial and nonfinancial objectives, commercial and noncommercial objectives. Second, even if the original social objectives are reasonably clear and simple, over time the goals of the enterprise begin to multiply. Third, besides confronting a welter of goals that may be unreconciled and unreconcilable, public enterprise must also reckon with the possibility that these goals sometimes change with changes in government. Fourth, public enterprises are the target of a complex set of pressures emanating from government offices and interest groups. Fifth, they often operate in highly imperfect markets, and are frequently in a position to make choices in these markets.

Attempts to control public enterprises have taken on many diverse shapes (e.g., Floyd 1984; Aharoni 1986: Chap. 6). Two broad types of control mechanisms are discerned: external and internal (e.g., Aharoni

1986: Chaps. 6 and 8). Internal control refers to those at the apex of the organizational pyramid, the top-level management, and specifically the chief executives and the board of directors. External control refers to the whole array of mechanisms that structure the enterprise's environment and set the "rules of the game." Some of the more prominent types of external control mechanisms used are statutory controls; parliamentary controls; ad-hoc policy directives; the use of *contrats de programme* (contract programs) like in France; the setting of various financial parameters such as investment and pricing criteria, profitability and rate of return targets or external financing limits; nonfinancial performance indicators, such as consumer performance targets or managerial performance indicators; the introduction of market competition; and so forth.

Countries have oscillated between reliance on internal controls and very detailed external controls. Indeed, Britain provides an excellent example of the continuous and relentless struggle for control over public enterprise: From a beginning in which public enterprises were fully controlled by the government bureaucratic machinery, through a phase of almost laissez-faire when the predominant assumption was that the "responsibility for efficient management rested with the board" (Chester 1975: 961), followed a period of rapid and intensive growth of external control mechanisms adapted on an ad-hoc basis (e.g., Redwood and Hatch 1982; Curwen 1986). The transition from one phase to the other was spurred by the conception that the existing controls were inadequate: either that there was too little autonomy, or that there was too little control.

As the British experience and the experience of other countries indicate, many of the external controls have failed to achieve the intended results (e.g., Redwood and Hatch 1982; Vernon and Aharoni 1982; Curwen 1986; Prosser 1986; Aharoni 1986: Chap. 6). To cite a recent research report on Britain: "The pattern that emerges throughout is one of piecemeal solutions to perennial problems ... whilst the control mechanisms grow in complexity their utility declines" (Redwood and Hatch 1982: 23). At times, an invidious glance is cast by the British toward some of their European neighbors whose control systems seem to work better, when viewed from across the channel. For example, a research study carried out for NEDO (National Development Office) emphasizes the importance of learning from the experience overseas and cites France as an example of conflictless and "fruitful interchange of knowledge and views between government and enterprise" (Garner 1976: 33). Yet, from the perspective of a less distant observer, in France relationships between public enterprise and government are far from being as harmonious and as conflictless as depicted, and the problem of controlling public enterprise is far from being solved (e.g., Anastassopoulos 1981).

At times the view prevails that the solution to all the nagging and seemingly insoluble problems of control is privatization. As one writer puts it, one motive for the recent drive for privatization has been "world-weary anxiety to be rid of the problems of controlling nationalized industries by being rid of the industries themselves" (Kay and Silberston 1984: 78). Yet, most researchers are indeed very skeptical about the wisdom and widespread applicability of this solution (e.g., Redwood and Hatch 1982; Heald 1984, 1985; Curwen 1986; Prosser 1986; Aharoni 1986).

The difficulties in achieving a satisfactory measure of control over public enterprise through external mechanism, and the limitations of privatization, redirect attention toward internal control and those at the apex of the internal control pyramid – the board of directors and top-level management. Can *they* be trusted to navigate the public enterprise successfully toward fulfilling its multiple goals and achieving a satisfactory measure of efficiency – and under what conditions? This once prominent subject in discussions about the control of public enterprise, seems to have been sidetracked and left somewhat in the shadow in the past decade. Perhaps the reason lies in some disillusionment with the workings of the board, especially where it enjoys a relatively great amount of autonomy (like in Britain) and the consequent search for better alternatives. From this latter perspective the external control mechanisms (as yet unexplored at the time) had perhaps more appeal than rethinking the issue of internal control. Rethinking this issue obviously involves dealing with difficult human-material questions, such as what are the appropriate selection criteria, modes of organization, and incentive systems for ensuring the proper functioning of those placed at the top of the internal control pyramid in public enterprise. Unavoidably, as will become clearer further on, this means coming to grips with such difficult, intangible, and slippery issues as motives, predispositions, perceptions, and action-inclinations. In comparison, the external control mechanisms may look far more tangible, graspable, and manageable, and hence more appealing to those decision-makers struggling with the problems of controling public enterprise. Yet, the failure of many external controls suggests that perhaps coming to grips with the difficult questions presenting themselves in relation to internal control is after all a worthwhile endeavor. In resuming the struggle with these questions it seems futile and wasteful to re-embark on the old well-travelled tracks: As the following chapter shows, most past discussions on the subject, while led by well-informed, close-to-the-scene, and keen observers of the public enterprise, had little empirically solid foundation to lean on. While the issues at stake are well-exposed, and the solutions suggested well-intended, their appropriateness is rarely examined through systematic and vigorous empirical research. The study presented in the following chapters was guided by the belief that the gap created by the lack of a solid empirical foundation needs to be filled and that the solution-seeking process needs to be infused with some factual data before real progress can be made.

Chapter Two
Controversy Over the Board of Directors

Most public enterprises in the mixed economies are legally organized as corporations, either as public corporations or as publicly owned corporations. The corporate form of organization is intended to allow the public enterprise a larger amount of autonomy than that of the government department. In contrast to the latter, the enterprise organized as a corporation is not subject to annual legislative budgetary appropriations, is allowed to accumulate funds, is not subject to civil law regulations in its employment policies, and is subject to fewer day-to-day government directives. The greater amount of autonomy also finds expression in the fact that the direct control over the enterprise is put into the hands of an autonomous body, the board of directors, rather than being in the hands of government officials. Yet, beyond the relative uniformities in legal organization, and beyond the general will of governments to grant the public enterprise a greater amount of autonomy and discretion than that enjoyed by the government department, there are great variations in the actual modes of control and management of the public enterprise in various countries. The variations are partly due to the specific conditions prevailing in each country: its culture and historical heritage, its political milieu, its stage of socioeconomic development, and so forth (e.g., Aharoni 1986: Chap. 11). Partly, however, the variations are due also to the wide differences in the ideologies, philosophies, and basic conceptions about how best to control the public enterprise. These differences have, among other factors, led to different responses to a problem common to all public enterprises. This problem is how to reconcile the aim of economic efficiency with other aims dictated by the public interest; how to achieve a measure of autonomy in their management while at the same time subjugating them to public control (e.g., Maniatis 1968; Shepherd 1976: 33–47; Stefani 1981; Sexty 1983).

Almost every nation – whether it is developed or developing and whether its governmental philosophy calls for maximum use of public or private enterprise, and regardless of its form of organization – has been, or is now confronted with the problem of reconciling the requirements of public enterprises for operating and financial flexibility with the need for controls to assure public accountability and consistency with government policy (Seidman 1970: 156).

The difficulties encountered in achieving such reconciliations are well reflected in the controversy about the structure and functions of the board of directors in public enterprise.

A full understanding of the controversy requires a closer look at the two major elements, the "public" element and the "enterprise" element, and at the major foci of tension arising from their combination. We turn now to a brief review of these.

The Public Element and the Enterprise Element: A Definition and Analysis of Foci of Tension

In an attempt to conceptually define the "public" element and the "enterprise" element, Ramanadham (1984) comes up with the following definitional criteria. In relation to the "public" element three factors are of major importance:

1. Nonprivate accretion of net benefits. The net benefits of the activity undertaken by the enterprise do not go to the enrichment of a private group of individuals standing in the position of owners.
2. Public decision-making. Entrepreneurial and other decision-making activity shifts from the level of private groups of persons brought together as owners and/or managers to some public level. The shift, says Ramanadham, is not just the product of government ownership but is rather "justified squarely by the intrinsic relevance of non-private criteria in decision making" (1984: 9). And further, "the essential aspect of a public decision is not that the government ... makes it, but that the decision rests on distinctive social criteria" (1984: 9).
3. Social accountability. The enterprise is accountable to the public for its performance. Says Ramanadham: "The accountability requirement is closely linked with the element of public decision ... and has to be established in relation to the criteria that underlie the relevant public decisions" (1984: 13).

Ramanadham discerns two parts in the anatomy of the social accountability concept:

[F]irst, there is the accountability of the managers provided with certain powers and privileges, responsibilities and duties, objectives and targets, resources and directives. . . . Then there is the other part, viz., the accountability of the enterprise to society. Here enterprise is a comprehensive term and, in the context of the public sector, covers both the managers and the outsiders who play a role in the decisional process . . . it extends to the totality of the operations of the enterprise, whichever source the decisional bases have been derived from, from the multiple angles of the consumers, the workers, the public exchequer, economic growth and social transformation (1984: 14–15).

In relation to the "enterprise" element there are two factors of major importance:

1. Financial viability.

This is best understood as an expression, in brevity, of a conscious effort on the part of the enterprise toward raising a net revenue.

. . . The 'viability' feature has to be spelt out as viability *by intention* and *in the long run* . . . or else it is not an enterprise and, in the public sector context, may be defined as non-enterprise activity of a government agency (Ramanadham 1984).

2. The cost-price equation. Here the concern is with the way in which financial viability is achieved. The enterprise is supposed to go by cost considerations in determining the payments that customers are to make for its products/services. Here:

[E]xtreme caution is needed before a disproportionate excess of price over cost (or shortfall below cost) in the case of a given output is practised, for it is open to challenge by consumers adversely affected (Ramanadham 1984: 23–24).

The two aspects are difficult to reconcile. As a review of the literature shows, the foci of tension pervade all the major areas of management, from policy formulation to performance assessment. In more detail, they reveal themselves in the following areas.

The Policy-Making Process. The two aspects imply a different orientation. Maintaining financial viability in the long run implies an orientation toward market forces and economic opportunity. This means adapting to prevalent market conditions, exploiting economic opportunities, and taking calculated risks to ensure and enhance long-term financial viability.

The public aspect, on the other hand, implies an orientation toward the public interest. In concrete terms, public enterprises have been found to be expected to contribute to the following sociopolitical goals: regional development, services to remote areas, technological innovation and pace-setting in industry, cross-subsidization, i.e., supporting other domestic enterprises, maintaining full employment, controlling inflation, controlling strategically important industries, developing socialist consciousness (e.g., Monsen andd Walthers 1980; Aharoni 1986).

Quite often the two types of orientation conflict with each other: Public-interest considerations very often imply a cost in terms of financial viability (and vice-versa). For example, refraining from employee dismissal in times of economic recession, providing transportation to remote and sparsely populated areas, establishing a plant in a newly developing area with inadequate infrastructure, and so forth. The different time horizons implied in the two orientations are also a source of tension and conflict. Maintaining financial viability in the long run implies the adoption of a strategy directed toward future trends: planning ahead and gearing resources toward future opportunity structures. On the other hand, quite often, the public interest requires attention to immediate social problems. For example, maintaining financial viability in the long run may require the adoption of a capital-intensive technology, whereas pressing current employment problems may exert pressure toward the adoption of a labor-intensive technology.

The Decision-Making Process. The two aspects involve the application of different decision criteria. In the one case, the major decision rods are profitability, financial soundness, and economic efficiency. The basic ingredients are cost-benefit calculations in economic terms. In the other case, the major decision rods are the contribution to the general welfare and to the ultimate objectives of the country. This means the application of social cost-benefit criteria: weighing the social benefits and social costs among themselves and weighing the social benefits against the social costs.

Tension arises not only because of the need to apply different decision criteria but also because of the different *nature* of the basic decisional frame of reference. Economic rationality implies a stable frame of reference: the formulas applied are the same over time, only the input parameters change. The application of social cost-benefit criteria, on the other hand, implies an ever-shifting frame of reference due to changing social conditions, changing political power structures, and changing values. The major difficulty here is that managers faced with the task of efficiently organizing and coordinating organizational resources toward achieving the specified goals find it difficult to function under conditions of ever-changing frames of reference.

The Staffing of Top-Level Decision-Making Positions. The two aspects require different types of knowledge and expertise. Maintaining financial viability in the long run requires appropriate managerial, financial, and entrepreneurial skills. Quite often these do not go together with the knowledge and skills required for serving and advancing the public interest, such as being well attuned to the goals of the dominant political elite or to the needs of the community being served, or having the ability to mediate between and reconcile conflicting interest groups.

The Managerial Climate. The two aspects imply a different managerial climate. Achieving commercial success and maintaining financial viability in the long run imply a substantial measure of managerial autonomy. Public decision-making and social accountability, however, are wide open to constant outside pressures from a great variety of interest groups, political or otherwise. The major difficulty here is that a management required to be responsible for maintaining the enterprise's financial viability in the long run may feel impaired in its ability to do so under a climate of openness toward a variety of different pressures.

Managerial Performance Evaluation. The two aspects imply the application of different criteria for evaluating managerial performance (e.g. Sexty, 1983: 29). The enterprise aspect requires the application of a variety of commercial, financial, and economic success criteria. The public aspect, on the other hand, requires the measurement of managerial performance in terms of how well various social objectives have been implemented. There are two major difficulties here. One is the difficulty of quantifying the progress made toward achieving various social objectives and bringing the measures to a common denominator with the economic objectives. The other difficulty is that it is extremely difficult in many cases to allocate the division of costs between commercial and non-commercial goals, as is necessary for measuring each type of performance.

Questions Arising in Relation to the Board of Directors in Public Enterprise

The debate about the structure and functions of the board of directors in public enterprise revolves around the question of finding the best ways and means for organizing the top-level decision-making process in public enterprise, so as to achieve the best possible balance, and minimize the tension between the enterprise and public elements.

This is essentially a debate over a public choice issue emanating from the fact that in public enterprise, decision-making is shifted to the public level, and decisions need to be made as to how to organize this process. The debate reflects well the tensions mentioned above. It centers around several major questions. Who shall be the decision-makers? What recruitment and selection criteria should be applied for selecting the board membership? At the core of these questions is the fact that the enterprise and public aspects imply different basic orientations. Several issues are involved here:

1. Can the same persons be responsible for and represent adequately both aspects, or is it necessary to divide responsibilities between different persons or bodies?

2. Who shall represent the public interest? Can the government as "owner" of the resources and net benefits adequately fulfill this role? If yes, how and under what conditions? If not, who can? Some of the difficulties presenting themselves have been well exposed by Aharoni (1982: 69) in his essay on "State-owned enterprise: an agent without a principal":

> The state is not a person, not even a single organization. It acts through a variety of ministers, legislators and civil servants, who are themselves agents of the general public. These different agents invariably see their mission as different from one another.
>
> ... Their decisions are influenced by all sorts of interest groups – consumers, labor unions, and others – all of which claim at least some right to participate in the process of goal formulation.

In such an amorphous situation how can a public interest representation be really ensured? But more than that:

> SOE (state owned enterprise) managers may question the legitimacy of demands from government because they perceive the real "goals" of the amorphous principal – the state – to be different. The government may require the SOE to avoid price increases to combat inflation, to procure locally made and more expensive goods or to maintain the size of its labor force to secure employment, or to pursue certain objectives perceived as important in achieving a short-term political gain. In all these cases, managers may have different perceptions of the legitimate role of the enterprise (Aharoni 1982: 71).

Moreover, Howard (1982) who shares Aharoni's skepticism of relying on the government as sole arbiter of the public interest, maintains that social accountability *requires* the introduction of controls from outside the government. In his view state and market controls are not sufficient for making public enterprises accountable for their impact on society. What is needed is a "fiducial relationship between the public enterprise and individuals and organizations in the community sector" (Howard 1982: 92). Such relationship involves "participatory controls, bearing on matters such as impact on local community, quality of work conditions, quality of products and services, quality of environment, economic security, job opportunities and training, and so on" (1982: 89).

3. Given the necessity for both, expertise and experience, required by the enterprise aspect, and a "broad view", required by the public aspect,

what terms of appointment should be applied? Should appointments be made on a full-time basis, which is likely to further experience and expertise, or on a part-time basis, to allow for an "outside view" – or a combination of both? In the latter case, what is the appropriate "mixture"? Should appointment be made for relatively long periods of time, to allow for an accumulation of experience, or for a relatively short term, to ensure "neutrality"?

4. Given the intricacies of decision-making processes, what are the best ways to structure these processes, so as to ensure that both the public-interest criteria as well as the economic efficiency/profitability criteria will be applied, and will be applied in the "right way" at the "right time" to the "right issues"? Should the board act mainly in a *legitimating* capacity, i.e., in a role that is "generally passive and simply fulfills the requirements of the corporate charter" (Waldo 1985: 17) or should the board fulfill a *directing* role, i.e., focus on the enterprise's future goals and on the strategies by which they will be reached? In the latter case, exactly what should be the decision issues dealt with on the board and what should be those dealt with on the managerial level? Or, in other words, what decision issues should be defined as falling into the "goal and strategy" category and what as falling into the "day-to-day management" category?

5. Given the requirement for a measure of managerial autonomy, on the one hand, and the requirement for public control, on the other hand, what are the best ways for achieving both? This question is closely related to the above question of allocating decision-making powers between the board and management. The central question here is what decision issues should be left to the management so as to satisfy the condition of a required amount – what is it? – of managerial autonomy?

The details of the debate, its bases, and the proposed solutions will gradually emerge as we present a series of models, as advanced by various proponents, for the structure and function of the board of directors in public enterprise.

The Major Models for the Board of Directors in Public Enterprise

Since the public corporation in Britain is considered to be one of the most serious attempts to achieve the desired balance between autonomy and control in public enterprise, it is perhaps convenient to start with the basic conceptions of Mr. Morrison of the British Ministerial Cabinet – "the principal architect of the modern public corporation" – and of others close to him in thought, and to gradually proceed to more contrasting conceptions.

According to Mr. Morrison the board should be vested with full authority regarding the day-to-day management of the corporation, as distinct from policy matters which should be subject to ministerial and parliamentary control. The major rationale for this division is that "A large degree of independence for the boards in matters of current administration is vital to their efficiency as commercial undertakings" (Morrison 1947).

Recognizing the difficulties involved in maintaining in daily life a strict division between matters of policy and routine management, Morrison expected the parties, mainly the board and the responsible minister, "to be conscious of their legal rights: the legal right of the Minister to give general directions or to withhold approvals, and the legal rights of the board within the field of day to day management" (Morrison 1954: 264). Being aware that the autonomy granted to the corporation could be misused to further "this or that sectional interest," Morrison emphasized the importance of the board's complete dedication to the public interest:

It [the public corporation, M.D.] must have a different atmosphere at its Board table from that of a shareholders' meeting; its Board and its officers must regard themselves as the high custodians of the public interest (Morrison 1933: 156–157).

Important in achieving this orientation by the board toward the public interest is the elimination of the profit motive. "The public corporation" wrote Morrison, "must be no more capitalist business, the be-all and end-all of which is profits and dividends, even though it will, quite properly, be expected to pay its way" (Morrison 1933: 157).

The structure of the board should match its functions. The board should be composed of men with "drive, imagination, insight, and the capacity for grasping large questions of policy." Expertise and the ability to take "a broader view" should be the qualifying criteria for membership. A good combination of both could be achieved by a "mixed board composed of full-time and part-time members; in which the full-time members have special responsibilities without being heads of departments; while the part-time members are men of wide experience brought in from outside the industry in order to look at its problems with a more detached view" (Robson 1962: 228).

Impartiality is essential and appointments on political or any other partisan grounds should be avoided (e.g., Robson 1962: 217, 219). According to Robson, "If appointments are made on political grounds, a spoils system is likely to come into existence which will weight heavily against the national interest" (1962: 219). Appointments for life should be avoided, since this is likely to reduce both ministerial control and parliamentary influence over the public corporation (Clegg 1955: 273). Thus, one desirable aim, continuity of top management, should be balanced against another desirable aim, that of governmental and parliamentary responsibility. Economic efficiency is not the sole consideration; there are other considerations to be taken into account, mainly that of safeguarding the public interest.

A different stand has been taken by Lord Wythenshawe (1957), according to whom the sole function of the board in nationalized industries is to ensure their economic efficiency. Since the parliament is utterly unfit to deal with this matter it should be left entirely to the board. A similar view has been taken by the Herbert Committee which maintained that boards should take into account only purely economic considerations. Considerations pertaining to the public interest should be left to government which should be able to give instructions to the boards to shape their policies accordingly.

The structural implication of these conceptions about the functions of the board is that it should be composed of functional directors, people who are experts in the particular field of management, who should be appointed for life.

A basic assumption of the proponents of the commercially oriented board is that such an orientation provides a clear set of objectives toward which managerial effort can be harnessed, and that it ensures the necessary incentives for managerial initiative and effort (e.g., Maniatis, 1968). Thus, the answer to those who worried, in connection with the Morrisonian conceptualization, about what will replace "the pervasive, intimate and powerful compulsions of the profit and loss system" (Salter 1952: 231), was that it is best not to replace it. The sharp division between the economic and noneconomic spheres of policy-making is also intended to draw a clear line between the sphere of ministerial control and the province of managerial autonomy (e.g., Maniatis, 1968). The safeguarding of this autonomy has been a constant worry for those who have thought that such autonomy is absolutely essential for managerial enterprise and initiative and for a sense of corporate responsibility (e.g., Davies 1963: 110–112); Reith 1956: 42–43). If the corporation is regarded as a strictly commercial undertaking, many questions would answer themselves and the minister would be involved with few policy questions. Conversely, "The further our conception is departed from," they cautioned, "the more policy questions will the minister have to decide" (HMSO 1956).

A major argument against the commercially oriented board was put forward by Tivey, who has written:

[I]t may be doubted if this doctrine provides a real answer to the problem. Social and political considerations are not occasional occurrences: they pervade the whole conduct of industry. Moreover, the points at which they arise are not always national in scope: they are often local or individual. National rulings about social standards need to be interpreted, therefore, by managers well down the industrial hierarchy. To declare a doctrine of 'commercial operation only' is to preempt the social decisions of these managers.

Again, the decision of the Government on social matters cannot fail to be influenced by the attitudes of the Chairman of public corporations. Ministers ... will not be helped to wise decisions if they are confronted by the industries' universal hostility to all social claims. . . . The situation therefore calls at least for understanding and discrimination about social matters by the management of the industries themselves (1973: 198).

Against the various views which attach high functional importance to the autonomous board in the process of policy formation, there are those who maintain that since the public enterprise does not have shareholders in the ordinary sense and since the minister is ultimately responsible for its policy, no real role is left for the board (Seidman 1970); this was the view taken, for example, by the Hoover Commission in the United States (1949).

Hanson (1965), in discussing the organization of public enterprise boards in developing countries, addresses himself to this view and asks ". . . [I]s there any point, in view of the Minister's policy forming responsibilities, in having a *Board* as well as a management team? Could not the whole pattern of organization and control be simplified and rationalised by eliminating it?" (1965: 400).

In his view an important function for boards in public enterprises in developing countries, which tend toward excessive administrative centralization, is that of serving as a "buffer" between governmental authority and operational management. Only "a strongly organized board, equipped with full authority over the enterprise except in those matters which are specifically reserved for ministerial approval" could fulfill this function (1965: 403–404). MacMahon (1963: 164) too maintains that the board in public enterprise is very important as a safeguard for its autonomy; it is a substitute for direct ministerial intervention and a means for isolating the corporation from political influence.

In Dimock's view (1949) there is "an important area of sub-policy and decision making midway between the overall action of Congress and the point where the administrator takes up." In Dimock's view "It is this area that a representative and resourceful board of Directors must occupy if government corporations are to operate with efficiency and accountability." According to this view, boards should concentrate on decisions relating to internal organization and procedures necessary to give effect to general government-set objectives.

Appleby (1956: 54–55) believes that since policy-making should be left in the hands of those ultimately responsible for the public interest, there is no place for an independent and impartial board. His recommendation for the organization of public enterprises in India was that the boards should be composed of (a) the general manager of the enterprise and (b) high officials of other enterprises and of ministries "with related, supervising and coordinating interests." Thus composed, boards can become "effective organs of governmental coordination, the members definitely empowered to speak for their respective ministries and capable of judging which matters should, in spite of delegation, be referred to higher authority." Appleby rejects, thus, the view that boards should not consist predominantly of civil servants. Indeed, he insists that they *should* because "those most attuned to public responsibility ... will generally but not always, be civil servants" (1956: 39). Thus, the rationale for a board composed of civil servants is twofold. First, it is assumed that civil servants are most likely to be able to represent the public interest. Second, it is contended that civil servants coming from various related ministries are also most capable of fulfilling the necessary coordinative functions between the various governmental bodies.

The idea that the boards should be composed of the representatives of various interests, not only of government, was adopted, for example, by France and Germany. In France, the board composed of representatives of three interests – the state, the employees, and the consumers – is the leading principle in the organization of the boards of public corporations. The tripartite conception of the governing board was formulated by the CGT [Compagnie Générale Transatlantique] as an alternative to "etatization." Similarly, Germany has workers' representatives on the governing boards of its public corporations. The appointment of government officials or of representatives of interested parties has been severely criticized. A main criticism has been that such appointments are likely to hinder the pursuit of consistent managerial courses and impede the development of corporate responsibility among the members of the board (e.g.,

Hanson 1965; Robson 1962: 217). "The effect of managerial initiative," says Hanson, "can be particularly serious" (1965: 377). Finnegan (1954) maintains that in France the boards composed on a partisan basis, instead of fulfilling their function as "buffers" between the corporation and the government, have become so weakened by conflicting interests that the field has been laid wide open to power struggles between the minister, his officials, the board, and management. In practice, Delion (1963: 121–124) contends that the board in France has lost its influence on management since the general manager instead of relying on support from the board tends to be in conflict with it. As a result he either tries to circumvent the board and deal directly with the minister or to encroach upon the board's authority.

Analysis

Our review indicates that the controversy about the functions and structure of the board in public enterprise revolves mainly around the three closely interrelated issues of its responsibilities, its relationship with government, and its composition.

A closer examination of the argumentation underpinning the various views reveals that the controversy stems largely from a series of divergent, explicit or implicit, assumptions concerning the behavior and motivation of those who would carry the responsibility for the conduct of the enterprise. We turn now to examine these assumptions as they relate to the central issues under debate.

Concerning the first of these issues, the nature of the board's responsibilities, views diverge, as we have shown, as to whether the board could and should be entrusted with major policy-making functions, or not. On the one hand, there are those who believe that the board should be entrusted only with subpolicy functions. On the other hand, those who believe that the board should play a major role in policy formation are divided among themselves between those who argue that its responsibilities should be confined to economic efficiency, and those who maintain that it should also cover matters of public interest – within its statutory duties.

A major assumption of those who maintain that the board should be responsible for the public interest as well as for commercial efficiency is that top-level managers could and would equally orient themselves toward, and be motivated by, both objectives. According to Robson:

One must not go to the ... extreme of insisting that the economic calculus shall dominate the minds and thoughts of the board ... to the exclusion of everything else. (1962: 427).

To expect a board of men of outstanding ability and long experience to draw a sharp line between the commercial aspects and the wider considerations which have a bearing on many important questions of policy, and to deny themselves the right to take the latter into account in their deliberations, is little short of absurd. The idea that they should do so is quite unrealistic (1962: 298).

A similar view, with a somewhat different intonation, may be found in the Nora Report in France, which argues that the state

"must actively seek to place the public enterprises under the leadership of persons who not only are devoted to the pursuit of the general welfare but also have high and well-established levels of competence in industrial and commercial management. The range of its choices should be as wide as possible" (Nora, 1967).

In dealing with the incentives which could replace the profit motive Robson says:

The public service motive will undoubtedly count for much – if we can awaken it. And so too will the stimulus of social esteem ... (1962: 454).

Those who favor a board oriented primarily toward commercial efficiency do not agree with the above assumption. In their view there is no real and adequate substitute for the "powerful compulsions of the profit and loss system" for harnessing managerial effort and for providing the necessary incentive for managerial initiative. Economic principles, it is maintained, provide clear criteria which are an absolute requisite for efficient managerial performance. First, they supply top-level management with clear criteria to guide it in its policy-making functions; in the absence of such clear norms a situation of anomie, or normlessless, is likely to develop and unity of purpose would be difficult to achieve. An anomic situation, it is maintained, is detrimental for the morale of management, and involves a loss of much managerial energy on efforts to reach consensus about policies.

Second, economic principles provide clear measuring rods for evaluating managerial performance, without which it is doubtful whether full managerial efficiency could be achieved.

Third, the principles of commercial efficiency are relatively easy to adapt and reinforce throughout the administrative structure of the organization, which is an absolute condition for achieving organizational efficiency. On the whole, those who advocate a purely commercial orientation for the board doubt whether the public interest could provide the necessary motivation for top-level management and whether it could supply adequate criteria for the achievement of effective managerial and organizational performance.

At the core of the second major issue, the nature of the board's relationship with government, is the question of managerial autonomy. While nobody seems to much dispute the contention that a measure of autonomy is necessary to stimulate management toward enterprise and initiative, and that, on the whole, management will resent, and feel frustrated by government intervention in the affairs of the corporation, views diverge as to the weight which ought to be given to this consideration against others, and also, as to the ways of achieving a measure of autonomy.

First, it is doubted by some whether a large degree of autonomy is a unanimous blessing. These doubts are rooted in the assumption that selfish interests are a powerful motive behind human action and that managers in public enterprise would be no exception to this rule; an autonomous management, it is assumed, could divert the corporation from objectives, economic or otherwise, dictated by the public interest toward objectives stemming from selfish interests.

In its extreme form, this argument leads to the contention that public enterprise should not be left in the hands of autonomous boards and that control should be placed largely in the hands of those who are directly responsible for the public interest, i.e., the government and other interested parties.

An opposite view is taken by the those who have a less pessimistic outlook about managerial motivation, who do not believe that self-interest would predominate in the minds and actions of top-level management, and who, in addition, believe that managerial autonomy is utterly important for the sound and efficient management of public enterprise. A division, however, exists between those who believe that a true measure of autonomy could only be achieved if commercial efficiency would be the dominant orientation of public enterprise, and those who contend that this is not an absolute must. The first maintain that governmental control and intervention are unavoidable if the enterprise is to be used for the implementation of various sociopolitical objectives, while the latter believe that social responsibility does not necessarily prevent the delineation of certain spheres of action for which the board would bear full responsibility, and within which it would be completely free of governmental control. In the latter case the major issue is what spheres should and could be left to the sole discretion of management. Few believe nowadays that the separation of "day-to-day management" from "matters of general policy" is a feasible and realistic solution (e.g., Robson 1962: 76, Chap. 6; Hanson 1962: 112, 214–215). Some, for example Robson (1962: Chap. 6) believe that the solution lies in two directions: (a) In certain spheres government control should be instutionalized and routinized through formal legal provisions (e.g., by providing for ministerial approval of certain actions). (b) In other spheres, which are "normally" left to the discretion of management, government should be able to exercise control only if it is willing to assume the responsibility for such control, i.e., through a published directive.

If this principle were to be accepted, there would be a notable reduction in the political element about wages and prices ... ministers would be reluctant to intervene on those occasions when electoral considerations, the prestige or popularity of the government, have been the chief motives for their interest in those matters (Robson 1962: 160).

Hanson, however, contends that

No formal grant of 'immunities' can ensure that the degree of freedom originally envisaged is in fact realized; for the corporation, being an organ of government, cannot, in the last resort defend its autonomy against a government determined to bring it under the harrow (1965: 343).

Although general guidance on the exercise of ministerial powers can be given in constituting legislation, ... the establishment of a just balance between autonomy and control is possible ... only through the development of appropriate conventions and understandings (1965: 370).

Concerning the third major issue of debate, the board's composition, two questions stand out as most important. One concerns the bases of recruitment of board members. The other, concerns whether and to what degree members should function on a part-time or, conversely, on a full-time basis.

The most-debated issue concerning recruitment is what criterion should be applied: should "impartiality" be the dominant criterion, or, on the contrary, should board members be chosen on a partisan basis? In essence the question is who should represent the "public interest." Should it be those who have a "direct interest" in the corporation, like the government, the workers' representatives, and so on? Or, would the public interest be better taken care of by an impartial body? Those who favor impartiality argue that this is the best way to safeguard the public interest. A major assumption underlying this argument is that members chosen on political or other partisan grounds would unavoidably orient themselves toward the interests of the bodies which they represent; their considerations and actions would be guided and dominated by narrow partisan interests rather than by the public interest. The board would thus be torn between the varying interest groups, with the result that policies would be formed on an ad-hoc basis, since it would be impossible to achieve the unity of purpose necessary for long-range policy-making.

On the other hand, those who favor partisan appointments argue that the public interest could be taken care of only if board members represent, in body, the various groups who have an interest in the corporation's activities. Apparently, the major assumption here is that it is necessary to control the actions of board members by, and make them responsible to, concrete bodies – each of which has an interest in the activities of the corporation – if a measure of action toward the public interest is to be achieved at all.

Impartial people, people who are independent of concrete interest groups, so the assumption seems to go, cannot be entrusted with the public interest. For how would they know what that interest is and what would motivate them to act in accordance with it? In addition, how would they be able to reconcile and balance the interests of their various "publics"?

The core argument for full-time membership on the board is that the managerial experience necessary to achieve a measure of economic efficiency is gained only gradually and through active involvement in the process of management. Since the logic of this argument can hardly be disputed, part-time membership must be justified by some special reasons. The prevalent argument is that part-time members would be able to take a "broader view" than full-timers. It seems that the hidden assumption on which this argument rests is that full-time membership and expertise are in some ways antithetical to the public interest. Indeed, those who maintain that the dominant orientation should be commercial efficiency are, as we have shown, in favor of a board composed of full-time members only – *appointed for life*. Only those who believe that the board should be equally responsible for both economic efficiency and the public interest favor part-time membership; they also oppose, in principle, appointments for life. The latent assumption seems to be that full-time membership carries with it a high degree of involvement and identification with the corporation which would motivate board members to prefer the interests of the corporation over those of the public. A similar logic seems to apply to expertise, i.e., expertise involves a narrowing of horizons which can be detrimental of the public interest. Thus, "a broader view" would mean the ability to "look at ... problems with a more detached view," i.e., the ability to detach oneself from the enterprise and its selfish interests, and to turn one's eyes toward broader issues of public interest. Indeed, at the extreme are those who do not see any disadvantage in a board composed of part-time members: only economic efficiency would be taken care of by "experts," the executive management, while a board composed of part-time members well-attuned to the public interest (either by directly representing various interested parties or by being nominated as public representatives) would formulate the overall policy of the enterprise, in accordance with that interest.

Obviously, the divergent assumptions exposed above constitute a weak link in the theory of the board of directors in public enterprise and only empirical research can provide the materials for some stronger foundations. Yet there is a set of assumptions that *unify* rather than divide those concerned with the conduct of the public enterprise, and these have an equally weak empirical foundation. These too need to be exposed and investigated because of their profound impact on theory. The most important set of such assumptions is found in relation to the issue of managerial autonomy. As we have seen, among all the parties involved there is great concern about this problem. At the root of this concern are certain more or less explicit assumptions about the potential impact of particular characteristics of the public enterprise on its active management. Thus, one prevalent assumption is that the multiplicity of goals characteristic of the public enterprise might have a negative impact on the sense of direction of its active management. There is widespread concern that the need to orient themselves toward multiple goals, some of which are ambiguous and some incompatible, will rob management of the much-needed sense of clear direction and will implant in it a sense of anomie (normlessness), or a sense of excessive freedom. For example, the proposal according to which the active management should be guided by only one set of goals (e.g., economic-commercial goals), while the implementation of other goals (e.g., social goals) should be ensured through "special" provisions, is guided among others by the will to eliminate a confusion over goals.

A second prevalent assumption is that the need for close public control to ensure the implementation of various social goals, and the resultant involvement of public agencies in the decision-making process, might have a negative impact on the sense of self-direction of the active management. There is widespread concern that the constraints imposed on the managers might result in a feeling, among them, that they lack the powers essential for adequately fulfilling their roles. As a consequence, their sense of self-direction might be impaired, giving way to a feeling of powerlessness or apathy. For example, the proposal according to which a broad operative area (e.g., the area relating to commercial and economic-efficiency matters) should be left to the sole discretion of management, is guided, among others, by the will to maintain a sense of self-direction among the managers, and shield it from such constraints as might impair its motivation to initiate and innovate.

A third prevalent assumption is that the exposure of the public enterprise to a variety of pressures and cross-pressures from various interest groups, might result in severe stress on the top-level active management and might thus impair its effective functioning. The will to shelter management as much as possible from exposure to such pressures is well-exemplified by the "buffer" concept of the board of directors in public enterprise.

Major Research Questions

Following the core issues delineated above, four lines of investigation seemed most promising. One is an examination of the actual goal orientations of top-level management. Such an investigation could throw some light on the much-debated question of managerial objectives. It could reveal the extent to which the *official* goals, commercial efficiency and the public interest, are also *effective* managerial objectives, i.e., the extent to which the top-level management actually identifies with these goals and adopts them as guidelines in their actions and decisions. It could indicate whether, and to what extent, managerial objectives are affected by self-interest, and the extent to which self-interest takes precedence over official responsibilities. It could help to clarify whether profitability is indeed, as assumed by some, a more powerful managerial incentive than social responsibility; whether it is indeed perceived by management as a more meaningful and organizationally adoptable objective than social responsibility.

Furthermore, a cross-sectional analysis, for example, comparing full-time with part-time board members, or government representatives with nonpartisan appointees, could reveal some of the contingencies affecting the goal orientations of various potential constituents of top-level management in public enterprise. The evidence thus produced could then support or, conversely, refute various assumptions about the behaviors and motivations of potential candidates.

A second line of inquiry concerns the attitudes of top-level management toward the complex of relationships between the corporation and government. In the present situation, students of public enterprise have little systematic empirical knowledge to lean on in these matters and must rely, as we have seen, on the largely impressionistic and simplistic assumption that "control" and "intervention" are resented by management and are detrimental to managerial initiative and enterprise. Such an assumption disregards the multifariousness of issues involved and does not leave room for the possibility that outside intervention and control in certain matters may be regarded by management as legitimate and may be willingly accepted by it. Concurrently, it also leads to a search for organizational solutions which would minimize and circumscribe government control as much as possible; solutions which, as indicated, seem unacceptable and unrealizable to many.

A detailed examination of the attitudes of top-level management concerning various facets of government control could reveal the areas where such control is considered as legitimate and is acceptable to management, and, conversely, where government control is likely to generate feelings of resentment and frustration among managers, and, consequently lead to conflictual relationships between the two. Such an analysis could then serve as a basis for better and more sensible solutions to what is considered as "One of the most difficult problems in the field of public enterprise [which is] to determine the degree and character of control which Ministers should exercise" (Robson 1962: 138). Or, at least, the analysis could reveal the direction in which, to use Hanson's words, "the development of appropriate conventions and understandings" between corporate management and government stands a fair chance.

A third line of inquiry concerns the role perceptions of top-level management. Such an analysis could indicate the extent to which role perceptions of top-level management match prescribed patterns, and the extent to which the actual workings of the board are in accord with the normative model underlying it. It could also clarify the extent to which the widely divergent assumptions about certain types of appointees to the board are grounded in reality. Thus, it could reveal whether part-time board members are indeed, as assumed by some students of public enterprise, more attuned to the public interest than full-time board members; and whether full-time board members are indeed inclined, as is assumed, to ignore the public interest in favor of narrow corporate interests.

A role analysis could elucidate the meanings attached to their roles on the board in general and to the "public interest" in particular, by board members recruited on a partisan basis, on the one hand, and those recruited on an impartial basis, on the other.

An examination of role perceptions could also expose the foci of role stress stemming from inconsistencies in self-role perceptions and mutual role perceptions among board members differing in modes of appointment (e.g., part-timers versus full-timers, representatives of various interest groups and those appointed on a nonpartisan basis, and so forth).

A fourth line of inquiry concerns an investigation of role-stress among the top-level active management in public enterprise. Such an analysis could indicate whether the various assumptions underlying the theorizing about managerial autonomy are indeed supported empirically. Specifically, such an analysis could indicate whether the top-level active management does indeed exhibit feelings of anomie, or normlessness, when faced with a conflicting goal structure and conflicting demands as to the conduct of the enterprise; whether it does indeed feel powerless and shows signs of apathy when faced with a situation in which the powers it actually possesses do not match those it perceives as essential for adequate role fulfillment; and, whether it does indeed experience role-stress when confronted with cross-pressures from various interest groups or when confronting a situation of conflict between the various interested parties.

Chapter Three
Some Existing Practices

In the previous chapter the various theoretical stances about the structure and function of the board of directors in public enterprise were exposed. The exposure highlighted the theoretical arguments for or against each model presented. The analysis following it focused on the weak links in the theories and proposed a framework for their research. What is still missing, however, is a perspective that will allow us to look at the models when implemented, and at the problems associated with their implementation. We believe that such a perspective can contribute toward a better understanding of the issues at stake; it can bring a dimension of concreteness into the discussion of these issues; and it can perhaps also expose some (new) aspects which were not at all or less apparent in the theoretical models. Here we wish to take advantage of the fact that among the great variety of organizational forms of the board of directors in mixed-economy public enterprises there are some that greatly resemble some of the models discussed, in order to look at these models "in reality."

We have chosen to focus on two cases that, in our opinion, can provide us with the desired insights. One is the board of directors in public enterprise in Britain, which was influenced a great deal by the Morrisonian conceptualization. The other is the board of directors in certain developing countries and also in Israel at the time of the research, which greatly resembles Appleby's model of a representative board. The choice of these cases was guided mainly by two considerations. One is the saliency of the cases. The other is the fact that they are extensively discussed in the literature, which is a basic requirement for our analysis. It is obviously not the individual case or country which we are interested in, but rather the basic features of some prevalent patterns that resemble some of the models discussed. Hence, wherever necessary, our descriptions will refer to a loosely defined "aggregate" that displays the features we are looking for. Our approach in each case will be to give a short schematic description of the existing pattern(s) which will be followed by a review of the major problems associated with, and critiques levelled against each, as these are reflected in the literature. These data will be referred to in our final chapter where a contingency perspective for the board of directors in public enterprise is proposed. The patterns described and the problems associated with them will be evaluated in light of this perspective.

The Morrisonian Model in Practice

Following the sequence of the theoretical discussion, we shall start with the board of directors in Britain which was greatly influenced by the Morrisonian conceptualization. A full description of the main organizational features of the board of directors in Britain is given in Chapter 4. Here we restrict ourselves to the most basic characteristics, which are as follows.

In Britain, the boards are structured and function according to the basic guidelines laid down by the specific statutes for public enterprises. These statutes specify that the boards should be appointed by the responsible minister on advice of the government. The statutory qualifications for membership are rather wide, but on the whole they emphasize as major bases for qualification experience in the particular (or in a related) industry and in one of the major managerial fields (e.g., finance, administration, manpower management). To ensure neutrality and avoid a clash of interests, members of the House of Commons and those engaging actively in commerce and industry are disqualified from serving on the boards. Members are appointed for a period of five years but may be dismissed by the responsible minister at any time if found unsuitable. The boards are typically composed of full-time members, many of whom are promoted to their position from inside the corporation, and part-time members, who come from outside the corporation.

The board is expected to control and give direction to the enterprise within the framework and terms specified by the statutes. According to the statutes the minister can give "directions of a general character... in relation to matters appearing to the Minister to affect the national interest" (SCNIO 1967/8). Such directions can be issued only after the minister has consulted with the board. The above powers of the minister are supplemented by particular provisions on particular topics such as major capital investments, reorganization, and so forth.

The above institutional framework was intended to isolate the boards as much as possible from direct ministerial intervention and to allow them to enjoy as much autonomy as possible. The members' role was meant to be one of directing and assisting the active management in its tasks, on the one hand, and of safeguarding the public interest, on the other.

A review of the literature on the board of directors in Britain reveals a number of problems. One major and prominent problem relates to ministerial control: There are many indications that the relationship between the boards and the responsible ministers is problematic and far from conflictless. The attempt to establish an "arm's length" relationship in the Morrisonian tradition has not met with much success. The problem was diagnosed as follows by the National Economic Development Office Report published in 1976 (NEDO 1976):

It seems to us that the wholly arm's length approach is based on a false analogy with the private sector... the issues of public policy involved are so large and politically sensitive that it is not realistic to suppose that they would even be left for long to management alone to determine, subject only to periodic checks on their financial performance.

The literature indicates that the problem is not unique to Britain. Moreover, it extends beyond major issues of public policy to more minor day-to-day matters, and it is compounded by the fact that quite often the ministers bypass the formal channels in their attempts to control the enterprise. Says Aharoni (1986: 226) in his extensive review of the public enterprise in the mixed economies:

In fact, in all countries of the world ... complaints abound that the minister intervenes directly in the day-to-day management of the enterprise... giving management direct orders and putting pressures on the firm to follow these directives, using the different powers of the ministry, including procrastination in the approval of the budgets, licences and so on. These directives are not given in a formal way but through what the select committee report called "lunch table directives".

The opinion has been expressed that such informal intervention is used by the ministers to circumvent responsibility, whereby "a minister cannot be held accountable for actions carried out by the firm in accordance with informal and therefore unrecorded directives" (Phatak 1969: 343). According to the literature, these informal political interventions seem to have a double-edged effect. On the one hand, they obviously impair managerial autonomy. On the other hand, however, they also appear to relax the control over the enterprise's management: "No chairman is going to be penalized for failure to reach his financial target when politics have been intervened" (Heath 1980). The tension arising from informal ministerial intervention is accompanied by: "a lack of trust and mutual understanding between those who run the nationalized industries and those in government (politicians and civil servants) who are concerned with their affairs" (NEDO 1976).

Moreover, the boards do not always tend to accept governmental control where this is made explicit:

Many of the reports and accounts from nationalized industries are concerned with a perennial debate about the control framework and the injustice of some particular feature of the regime imposed on them by Whitehall (Redwood and Hatch 1982. 43).

Anastassopoulos (1981), in an attempt to generally characterize the sources of conflict with government, maintains that in most cases conflict becomes acute where national objectives are at stake and further that "the possibility is endemic to the existence of two separate entities having two different purposes" (1981: 112).

The internal workings of the boards also show some signs of deviation from the patterns envisaged. Thus, some of the boards have been criticized for being in the habit of:

. . .not tackling their problems, but of minimising internal conflict at the expense of consumer or taxpayer, and of not living up to their role as 'high custodians of the public interest'. In particular, the part-time board members appear to have been reluctant to be critical of the administration as a whole, including the full-time members (Henney 1984: 48).

The proposition was put forth that the effectiveness of the part-time members is weakened because, among other things, their roles are not clearly defined and because they do not always have access to the information needed for effective role performance (Henney 1984: 48–49). A call has been sent out for:

A framework. . . to ensure that part-time board members understand and fulfill their proper role. . . The duties should be set forth in statute so that the question of their role does not have to be debated time and again around the board table, where differences of opinion will be muted to reach consensus,. . . (Henney 1984: 50).

There should be provisions made that would:

[E]nsure that they have sufficient information to monitor key aspects of board operations. . . in particular that they have sufficient information to be able to assure themselves that they are fulfilling their statutory duties (Henney 1984: 50).

The Appleby Model in Practice

A pattern akin to Appleby's conceptualization of a representative board is found in most developing countries. In India, for example:

All board members are nominated by the Government. It is a policy of the Government to appoint the secretary of the ministry that controls the firm concerned as the Chairman of the board of directors. An important nominated board member is the representative from the Finance Ministry. Representatives from other ministries who have an interest in the operations of the firm are also on the board. Retired civil servants, politicians defeated at the polls, ex-ministers, and a sprinkling of civilians complete the board membership (Phatak 1969: 340).

All in all "the boards of directors of Public Sector firms appear to be dominated by government officials" (Phatak 1969: 141).

Phatak describes the problems associated with the above arrangement as follows:

1. There is a high degree of instability of board membership: the large number of ex-officio board members are constantly in a state of flux, because being government servants, they are periodically subject to transfer from one department to another. Thus, many of the board members are not sufficiently familiar with the enterprise, its industry, and its internal management.

2. The enterprise is very vulnerable to ministerial intervention and control: The ministers use one or more board members as intermediaries who make certain that their wishes are implemented by the managing director:

The typical managing director of a public sector firm is subject to a continuous barrage of directives from the board members acting on behalf of the various ministries represented on the board. . . .[M]ost of the directives. . . are informal in nature and hence not recorded. . . .Ministers thus enjoy authority without the corresponding responsibility. . ." (Phatak 1969: 342–343).

3. Further, notes Phatak:

The smooth functioning of the board of directors is hampered because board members who are representatives of interested ministries attempt to bargain and emphasize the viewpoints of the ministers they represent (1969: 343).

4. Formal channels of communication are circumvented:

The formal organization structure of Public Sector firms requires the managing director to report to the chairman of the board of directors only. . . .[I]n actual practice the managing director receives directives from more than one person (1969: 343).

According to Phatak, public sector firms in India also suffer from a "man-"managerial vacuum" because of the absence of professional managers at the top echelon of the organization. This is due to the fact that top-management positions are filled "by recruitment from among those who have had administrative experience in the service, the armed forces, or other non-business institutions" (1969: 344), rather than by professional managers. This "has created an environment of anarchy in many Public Sector firms": workers do not stick to work schedules, absent workers are recorded as present, overtime is fictively recorded, and there is much overstaffing (1969: 344).

In Israel, where the boards were also composed partly of the representatives of various ministries and partly of the representatives of the "public at large," Aharoni (1970) observed some problems similar to those observed by Phatak in India. Thus, Aharoni found that most of the directors representing the various ministries saw their two tasks, their task in the ministry and their task as a director in a public enterprise, as complementing each other in the fulfillment of the ministry's policy; quite often, they were not guided in their decisions as directors in a public enterprise by the best interests of the enterprise. Rather, they saw the company as a tool for implementing the ministry's policy, whatever that was at the moment (Aharoni 1970: 92). Moreover, since the goals of the public enterprises were not clearly defined, the directors representing the various ministries used the enterprise for a variety of actions which were of interest to the ministry they were representing. Quite often, according to Aharoni.

[T]he enterprises are managed as a department of the Ministry, and the impression is that they are registered as ordinary companies only for reasons of convenience. In most of these cases... the Chief Executive is in fact subordinated to the major power centers in the Ministry (1970: 97).

The result is a rather conflictual relationship between the chief executive and the directors representing the various ministries, which has also some negative implications for the functioning and the long-term commitment of the chief executives to their roles:

The present situation in which the chief executives are required to carry out various special assignments while being accused at the same time by the public opinion and, quite often even by the Ministry, of not being profitable – does not encourage initiative among the Chief Executives and does not encourage them to stay on in their present jobs (1970: 375).

Ghai (1983) in describing the boards of parastatals in Africa, notes some other problems:

The civil servants who sit on the boards are senior bureaucrats who can devote only limited time to the affairs of the parastatals... Decisions are made more by the circulation of the file, which collects marginal comments as it winds its way around the corridors; initiative and aggressive policies are shunned in favor of caution and indecision . . .

The problem is aggravated by the rules whereby success is defined and rewarded, for these too travel over the department, so that the important consideration becomes the avoidance of risk and possible mistake. Promotion comes in due course if nothing untoward (albeit nothing spectacular either) has happened (1983).

Another problem noted by Ghai in regard to the boards of parastatals in Africa is that: "In many instances the governments do not have a coherent or clear policy towards or for the public sector. The governments do not know what they want of the public sector" (1983: 218).

In such a situation it is not surprising that there is a lack of accountability and that enterprises become irresponsible, says Ghai.

Summary. The preceding review indicates that in Britain, which adopted an organizational model that closely followed the Morrisonian conceptualization, the aim of confining political control to within the legally specified framework proved difficult, if not impossible, to achieve. The ministers use a variety of informal ways to impose their will, whether in regard to major issues of public policy or in more minor matters of day-to-day management. The boards in turn do not confine themselves to a passive resistance but rather take on an at-times militant position: The result is a "lack of trust and mutual understanding." Another problem area relates to the internal workings of the boards and especially to the part-time membership group: The part-time members, quite often, do not effectively enact their roles as custodians of the "public interest," and the will to minimize conflicts on the board leads to compromises at the expense of that interest.

In many of the developing countries, where boards are structured along lines akin to Appleby's conceptualization, the major problems addressed by researchers are mainly associated with the membership composition: The board members who are mostly recruited on the basis of their direct or indirect affiliation with the political, governmental, or administrative system open a wide door for direct and unobstructed political intervention and control and expose the enterprise's management to a variety of pressures and cross-pressures from the various interested parties. The board members also often lack any relevant managerial expertise and experience. Moreover, they bring into the enterprise's decision-making process an orientation that suits more an administrative bureaucracy than an enterprise struggling with the "hidden hand" of market forces. Their sometimes high rate of turnover, it is argued, does not allow them to acquaint themselves with the managerial problems facing the enterprise.

The problems associated with the "politicized" board in the developing countries seem to be of a different kind than those associated with the boards in Britain. In the developing countries, the problems reside in the membership composition of the board. They are thus inherent in the underlying model itself and cannot be disassociated from it. The major question posing itself here is why do the developing countries tend to adopt a model which so obviously subverts the "enterprise" aspects to the "public" aspect?

In Britain, however, the problems reflect a digression from the guiding model and the tensions arising out of this digression. The question arising here is why did the British not fully succeed in their attempt to isolate the boards from direct political intervention and why did they not fully succeed in their attempt to safeguard the "public interest" from within – through the boards' membership?

The above questions are in essence part and parcel of some more fundamental issues: (a) What explains the organizational patterns adopted by the various countries for the board of directors in public enterprise? Is it pure chance? A process of trial and error? Or, do some contextual factors explain these patterns, and if so, what are these factors? (b) What means do we have for evaluating the existing patterns and for deciding whether the choices made are "right" or "wrong"? (c) What perspective should we employ for deciding whether the problems associated with existing patterns can be solved, and what the solutions are?

The second and third questions have been asked from time to time in relation to various contexts. Usually those who have asked them had a rather definite perspective, a preferred theoretical normative model of the kind described in Chapter 2, which they applied when looking for the answers. Indeed, the extensive literature citations brought in when reviewing the problems associated with the patterns described for some of the developing countries allow us to take a glimpse at such an approach.

As to the first question, for those who are equipped with a preferred normative model which helps them discern "right" from "wrong", this question seems rather irrelevant. However for those of us, who take a skeptical view towards the prevailing normative models, all of the above questions remain open: We wish to come back to them when we have some answers to the questions posed in Chapter 2. This will be done in Chapter 10 where the findings of the present research are integrated into a suggested new perspective for looking at the board of directors in public enterprise, and where this perspective is used for evaluating the existing patterns described and the problems associated with them.

Chapter Four
Fresh Research in Britain and Israel

The Analytical Framework – General Outline

The research design was based on a number of basic considerations. First, it was clear that the issues to be investigated require a fairly large number of participants to make possible the required generalizations about the goal orientations, attitudes, and perceptions of various board membership groups. Hence, a study based on a limited number of cases seemed inappropriate. Second, it seemed reasonable to assume that the variables on which the research focuses, the goal orientations of board members, their attitudes toward government control in public enterprise, their perceptions about the role of the board of directors in public enterprise, and their self-role perceptions, may be influenced by a number of factors, partly related to the individual personalities and partly related to the context in which the individuals act. Given these assumptions, the research design had to be adapted to either highlight these factors or neutralize them as much as possible. While it may seem important and interesting to find out how certain individual characteristics or certain contextual characteristics such as type of organization affect the variables investigated, such investigation was outside the scope of the present research. Rather, the aim was to neutralize as much as possible the effect of individual characteristics and of organizational-context characteristics, and focus on the effect of those factors highlighted in the research problems defined in Chapter 2, i.e., the factors related to the various membership groups (insiders vis-à-vis outsiders; part-timers vis-à-vis fulltimers; members selected on a partisan basis vis-à-vis members selected on a neutral basis).

It was reasoned that a cross-sectional sample, i.e., a sample composed of members from various organizations and types of organizations, would neutralize, more or less, the impact of cross-organizational variances, whether this impact is direct or whether it is via recruitment and selection patterns typical to various types of organizations. It was also reasoned that the impact of individual characteristics that play no role in the recruitment, selection, and self-selection processes would be neutralized by random sampling: in a random sample traits would appear randomly and their influence would be neutralized through a process of mutual cancellation.

Third, it was reasoned that a cross-cultural design is needed for dealing with some additional factors that may influence the variables investigated. One such factor is the varying structure and function of the board of directors in various countries: Another factor calling for a cross-cultural design is the cultural milieu which, according to recent cross-cultural research on individuals in managerial positions, seems to have a significant effect on the role-related attitudes and perceptions of such individuals (e.g., Haire et al. 1966; Barrett and Bass 1970; Graves 1972; Hofstede 1980). Indeed, the two factors may not be completely independent of each other and they may even have some common roots such as the central value system of the society. Yet in any case, a cross-cultural design should be able to cover all major relevant cross-cultural variances.

Such coverage could then justify claims for the universality of findings, wherever applicable; or, conversely, enable a thorough elucidation of specificities. Such wide coverage was, however, not considered feasible in the present study. Instead, a more limited target was set: to compare two settings that differed substantially from one another, in an attempt to find out whether and where the differences had a significant impact on the variables studied. The settings and sample of participants are described in detail in the following sections.

The Settings

Every research project, notwithstanding the best intentions of the researchers, must endure many compromises due to constraints on time and resources. This project is no exception. As already mentioned, it would have been desirable to cover a wide variety of cross-cultural settings, yet compromises had to be made between the desirable and the feasible. The settings chosen were meant, within the limitations of our means, to provide as much variety as possible in relation to those factors considered to be most relevant to our study.

The choice fell on Israel and Britain, which, at the time the research was undertaken, displayed many of the contrasts we were looking for in the organization and underlying ideology of the public enterprise. We proceed now to describe separately each of the settings.[1]

Britain

State ownership of industrial and commercial undertakings in Britain has greatly expanded during the tidal waves of nationalization in 1946–1951 by the Labor Party. A series of Nationalization Acts in these years encompassed the airlines overseas and within the UK, the railways, canals and inland waterways, the London passenger transport system, a major proportion of the iron and steel industry, electricity supply, and the gas industry (Robson 1962: Chap. 3). The organizational vehicle of nationalization was in most cases the public corporation. The public corporation features the following principal characteristics (Robson 1962; Tivey 1973):

1. It is wholly owned by the state and has no shares and no shareholders.
2. It is a statutory body; its constitution, powers, and duties are prescribed by law and can be modified only by legislation.
3. As a body corporate it is a separate legal entity and as such it can sue and be sued, enter into contracts, and acquire property in its own name.
4. It is independent in respect to its actual operation and management, and has some degree of policy discretion. Its personnel are not civil servants and its finances are separate from those of the government.

Government Control. Each corporation is controlled by a particular minister, who has the power to appoint and remove the members of the board of directors.

The statutes generally provide for the minister to give "directions of a general character... in relation to matters appearing to the minister to affect the national interest." Such directions can be issued only after the minister has consulted with the board. The above powers are supplemented by statutory provisions on particular topics. The corporation must submit schemes of re-organization, substantial capital developments, training, and research for the minister's approval. The corporations are also required to provide the minister with such information as he requires. Additional matters subject to ministerial control include the management of reserve funds or surpluses. The Treasury has sometimes the right to be consulted on various matters, such as stock issues, the form of corporate accounts, the salaries of board members, and also the disposal of reserves and surpluses.

In regard to financial matters, the corporations are expected to shape their policies in accordance with some broad guidelines specified for them. In the early post-war years, general conditions were imposed by the government as follows. First, each industry was expected to break even "taking one year with another." Second, there was a condition that consumers should pay a price sufficient to cover the costs of providing the services consumed. In addition, the corporations were expected to serve the public interest through the provision of some services which, as in the case of transport services to remote areas, were deemed to be socially desirable even though they were clearly unprofitable. Within the framework of these conditions the corporation was free to conduct its business as it saw fit. In 1961 a white paper was introduced entitled "Financial and Economic Obligations of the Nationalized Industries." This stipulated (a) that the hitherto unspecified break-even period was to be fixed at exactly five years; (b) that out of earned revenues the nationalized industries were required to provide for depreciation at replacement cost, for future capital development, and for a contingency reserve to cover such matters as preventive obsolence, and (c) that financial objectives were to be introduced for each undertaking to be determined in the light of its own circumstances and needs. In general, these were to be expressed as a specified rate of return on capital employed which would vary between industries. The variance between industries was intended to make allowances both for the differing commercial viability of the various industries, and for differences in the degree to which they were required to provide unprofitable "social" services.

A further white paper was published in 1967 entitled "Nationalized Industries: A Review of Economic and Financial Objectives." The paper stated that "investment projects must normally show a satisfactory return in commercial terms unless they are justified on wider criteria involving an assessment of the social costs and benefits involved or are provided to meet a statutory obligation" (as cited in Curwen 1986: 59–60). The nationalized industries were required to utilize modern discounted cash flow methods of investment appraisal. A discount rate called the "test rate discount" (TRD) was specified for all nationalized industries equivalent to the "minimum rate of return to be expected on a marginal low risk project undertaken for commercial reasons" (White Paper 1967 Par. 9, p. 5).

The purpose of the white papers which, one should remember, have no legislative backing, was to obtain a better economic performance than just break-even. In the view of some, the above description "demonstrates a significant change in emphasis away from the idea that the nationalized industries existed primarily to serve the public interest and towards the idea that, since they operated in essentially the same way as large undertakings in the private sector, they should, like them, adopt economic criteria against which to judge their retrospective performances" (Curwen 1986: 57).

The Board of Directors. Board members are appointed by the minister on advice of the government. The chairman and deputy chairman are designated as such, i.e., they are chosen by the minister and not by their fellow members on the board.

The statutory qualifications for membership are quite wide. Usually the minister may appoint "persons appearing to him to be qualified as having had experience of, and having shown capacity in, industrial, commercial, or financial matters, applied science, administration, or the organization of workers." Thus, members may come from outside the industries concerned. Disqualifications of membership include: membership of the House of Commons, engaging in trade or business, and becoming of unsound mind.

There are no formal nominations for places on the board. Unions, stockholders, or customers have no right to have particular persons put on the board. Appointments are made for a limited period, most commonly five years. These may be renewed, and appointments are staggered so that entire boards are not changed at any one time. Board members may be dismissed by the minister. This may occur for reasons of alleged incapacity, neglect, or inefficiency; clearly, the minister can force resignation in cases of severe policy disagreement. In fact, many appointments are promotions of successful managers from inside the corporation, but there continues to be a significant group brought in from outside the corporation. It is also customary to appoint some part-time members to the boards. The proportion of full-time members to part-time members varies from corporation to corporation.

Israel

In contrast to Britain, state ownership of industrial and commercial undertakings in Israel is due mainly to a variety of pragmatic reasons, the most important of which are: the will to direct and accelerate economic development, security reasons, and the will to control industries of a monopolistic nature (Aharoni 1979).

In the first decade since the inception of the state in 1948, many of the public enterprises established were of the basic-industry type: in the extractive sectors, agriculture, and industry. The principal aims in establishing these industries were economic and the government stepped into these industries because of a lack of private funds and initiative. In the second decade, from 1958, the public enterprise sector expanded substantially and also covered fields of activity which were not of a basic-industry type:

developing the industrial sector, providing employment, and assisting regional development became additional important elements for the public enterprise sector. In not a few instances the involvement of the government, as a partner or owner, was due to the necessity to help with the financing of an enterprise or to prevent its bankruptcy. In the third decade beginning in 1968, a new phase is discernible: an effort is made to consolidate the public-enterprise sector. Many small enterprises are sold to private investors. Yet, at the same time, the government decides to expand into an almost equal number of new enterprises, mainly daughter companies of existing enterprises, or enterprises without equity capital.

The industrial and commercial undertakings wholly or partly owned by the state were formed under and governed by the General Corporations Ordinance.[2] Hence, they did not differ as legal entities from ordinary, nonpublic corporations. The general law obviously does not grant special rights to government as a shareholder unless specifically instituted in the corporation's articles of association.

The establishment of, or entry into a joint-stock corporation by the government was not subject in the first decade (1948–1958) to the approval of the entire government: each ministry could decide on its own to take up such activity. In 1958 a decision was passed by the government specifying that the establishment of any government corporation will have to have the approval of the Ministerial Committee for Economic Affairs. A government corporation was defined as "a corporation registered under the General Corporations Ordinance or under the Cooperative Association Ordinance, and which is wholly or partly owned and/or managed by the government; or, a corporation which was established by, or with the assistance of the Government." Still, this decision did not apply to the entry of the government into an existing corporation (even a "sleeping" corporation). In this respect the ministries were still free to act on their own, and, quite often, this was the way used by the various ministries to enlarge the scope of their activities.

As in Britain, a government corporation, as defined above, is usually placed under the auspices of the ministry(ies) whose spheres of activity are commensurate with those of the corporation. The responsible minister becomes the competent authority in all matters of concern to the state, and is responsible to the Israeli Parliament for the corporation's activities.

Government Control. The main vehicles of governmental control are the ministers and their representatives on the board of directors. In the first decade after the inception of the state, the ministers enjoyed a great deal of autonomy in dealing with the affairs of the enterprises under their auspices. In 1958, in an attempt to tighten control over the public-enterprise sector, the Ministry of Finance established the Corporations Office, afterwards called the Government Corporations Authority. Yet, as an extensive review shows (Aharoni 1979), this body had little influence over the public enterprises and the ministers until 1975, when the Government Corporations law was proclaimed, giving formal status to the Government Corporations Authority.

There are no formal provisions for the submission of periodic reports on the activities of the corporation to the minister, with the possible exception of annual or other reports distributed by the corporation among its directors. Yet, all capital investment projects are subject to governmental approval, usually represented by the ministry in charge of the corporation and the Treasury.

All corporations in which the government owns part of the share capital are liable to inspection by the State Comptroller who has the authority, after consulting with the Minister of Finance, to give directions to the corporation concerning its accounts and annual balance sheets. In accordance with the General Comptroller's Law (par. 10a), the objectives of control are to determine whether:

1. Expenses have been made in accordance with the official budget
2. Incomes have been derived according to the law
3. Incomes and expenses have been documented adequately
4. The actions under control have been carried out by the authorized personnel and in compliance with the law
5. The accounting, balance computation, cash and inventory control, and document management are efficient
6. The corporation's monies and assets are being adequately managed
7. Cash records and inventory records match the accounting records
8. The bodies controlled have "acted efficiently, effectively, and ethically"; an additional clause states that the Comptroller can also control "any other aspect – as he sees fit"

The following procedures were established by the government to ensure that enterprises will react adequately to the State Comptroller's Report. Where the government's share is 50% or more, the Report will be dealt with by a committee composed of the general manager of the responsible ministry, the board's chairman, the manager of the Government Companies Authority, and a representative of the Ministry of Finance. Where the share of the government is less than 50%, the Report will be dealt with

Table 4.1   Major differences between boards of directors in Britain and Israel

	Britain	Israel
Reasons for establishment	Mainly ideological	Mainly pragmatic
Regulation of activities	Special statutes	General Corporations Ordinance
Governmental control	Mainly through statutes and special directives, and through ministerial approval of major investment, reorganization, research and training schemes, and approval of the allocation of reserve funds	Mainly through government officials appointed to the board of directors and through the approval of major investments
Appointments to the board	By Minister responsible	By Minister responsible
Composition	Part- and full-timers appointed for limited periods. Most full-timers come from the ranks of managers within the corporation; part-timers are appointed on an impartial basis	Part-time membership. Members are appointed for limited periods. Many are high government officials; the others represent various interest groups or "the public at large"

by the board of directors in cooperation with a representative of the Ministry of Finance.

The Board of Directors. The board is appointed by the minister(s) in charge of the corporation. The chairman is designated as such by the minister(s). Usually, some of the board members are high officials in the ministry responsible for the corporation, or in the ministries related to its activities; it is assumed that they consult with the minister before endorsing important decisions. In addition to the members representing the ministries whose spheres of responsibility are related to those of the corporation, some of the members are representatives of "the public"; in case of a partnership, various members represent the various partners. Members representing the public may be chosen from among former high government officials; they may represent various interest groups, or they may be people with commercial, financial, or some other specific expertise.

Formally, members are appointed for a period of up to two years, but membership is often renewed and a substantial proportion of board members stay on the board for more than two years, most up to five years. Similarly to the case in Britain, appointments are staggered so that whole boards are not changed at any one time. The appointment of the general manager, himself a member of the board, is usually left to the board, but it is subject to the approval by the minister(s) responsible. All board members, apart from the general manager but including the chairman, function on a part-time basis, receiving nominal salaries or none at all. The major differences in the two settings are summarized in Table 4.1.

Target Populations and Samples

The basic aim was to include in the investigation all state-owned enterprises engaged in the production of goods or services and acting on a commercial basis.

In Israel this aim was indeed accomplished and the investigation comprises 17 corporations owned fully or partly (at least 50% of paid share capital) by the government and operated on a commercial basis (the full list of the corporations included appears in Appendix A).

In Britain we approached all the major nationalized industries but because the managements of three of them refused to cooperate it was necessary to settle for somewhat less than originally aimed at. Still, the final sample is more than just a probability sample of the British nationalized sector since it comprises almost all the major nationalized industries (the full list appears in Appendix A).

In relation to each of the corporations included, an attempt was made to compose a sample of the top-level management consisting of the chairman of the board, the chief executive, and a sample of board members. The latter were sampled so as to include those with most seniority on the board. An effort was made to include in each British case some part-timers as well as some full-timers and in each Israeli case at least one representative of each of the ministries represented on the board and at least one board member representing the public at large.

The total Israeli sample thus obtained consisted of 59 persons and the total British sample of 25 persons.

Procedures

Individual letters were sent to each of the persons included in the sample stating, in general terms, the aims of the investigation, and asking for an interview. The letter emphasized that the data obtained from the interviews will be analyzed in aggregate form and that the contents of the individual interviews will be kept confidential through all the stages of the investigation so that only the interviewer and the author will be able to identify the interviewees.

In Britain the chairman or the deputy chairman of the board was approached first, before all other full-time members. The letter asked for an interview with him and mentioned our intention to interview other board members as well. This type of approach generally precluded the possibility of approaching other full-time members whenever our letter to the chairman was encountered with a refusal to cooperate. Still, in some cases, we were able to approach the part-time members of enterprises whose chairman refused to cooperate so that the opportunity to contact at least some of the board members in these enterprises was not lost entirely.

Apart from the very few exceptions mentioned all the persons thus approached agreed to cooperate. An effort was made to schedule the interviews as close as possible to one another so as to minimize the chances of a changed "environmental climate" during the interviewing period.

In Israel, where several persons did the interviewing, it took about three months to complete all the interviews. In Britain, where all the interviews were carried out by a single person, the interviews stretched over a period of six months.

Data Collection: Sources and Instruments

The data collection methods had to be suited to the relatively large number of participants. Individual interviews with board members and a content analysis of board meeting minutes seemed to fit this purpose well. A more detailed discussion of the data collected and the instruments utilized follows.

The Interviews

The interviews were based on a structured questionnaire reproduced as Appendix B. The questionnaire was pretested on a small sample of board members. The questions and the underlying analytical rationale for each of them will be discussed in detail in the following chapters. At this point we present, for orientational purposes only, a schematic outline of the issues investigated and of the related main questionnaire topics (Table 4.2)

Table 4.2   Outline of issues investigated and related main topics

Issue of Investigation	Main Questionnaire Topics
Basic goal orientations	• Perceived goals of enterprise • Perceived criteria for resource allocation • Perceived raison d'être of the enterprise
Attitudes towards relationships with government	• Attitudes about using the enterprise for implementing government policies in various economic spheres • Perceived power relationships between the enterprise's management and government
Perceptions about the functions of the board and the roles of the various membership groups on the board	• Desired allocation of decision-making and legitimating powers between management/board/government • Perceptions about the actual power distribution between the various agencies determining the objectives of the enterprise • Perceptions about the functions of full-time and part-time members • Self-role perceptions

In addition to the questionnaire which was administered to all the board members interviewed, a ten-item questionnaire measuring role-stress, and reproduced as Appendix C, was used only in interviewing the chief executives in the sample.

The individual interviews lasted from about one and a half hours to about three hours, the average being about two hours. The interviewers were free to vary the sequence of the questions as they saw fit, and the conversation was allowed to flow as freely as possible during the interviews. Comments by the interviewees were recorded as they came along. In order to facilitate the recording of responses, prepared response categories were indicated on the questionnaire sheets used during the interviews, but these were used only when they accurately reflected the responses; otherwise responses were recorded as given.

The Minutes of Board Meetings

Apart from the interviews, an effort was also made to obtain the minutes of board meetings in order to study the actual decision-making process in the enterprises investigated. In Israel the State Corporations Authority put at our disposal the minutes of all board meetings of the corporations investigated. In practice we used only those minutes which contained a *detailed* transcription of the discussions held during the meetings, to perform a content analysis as described in detail Chapter 5. The purpose of the analysis was to investigate the criteria that are used by board members in resource-allocation decisions. The basic idea was that such an analysis was important for supplementing and cross-validating the data relating to the basic goal orientations obtained from the interviews.

Data Presentation

The presentation of the data follows the basic logic outlined in the Analytical Framework section. Comparisons are made to highlight the differences, if such exist, between the various types of membership groups and between the two settings.

Notes

[1] The field research was carried out in 1972 in Israel and in 1975 in Britain.
[2] In 1975, after the completion of the research, a Government Corporations Law was passed which in many respects changed the legal framework of the enterprises wholly or partly owned by the government. The description given below applies to the time of the research, before the introduction of the new law.

Chapter Five
Board Members' Goal Orientations

An analysis of goal orientations among the board membership should be able to clarify the following major questions. First, how far does the top-level management in public enterprise actually identify with its official guiding norms – commercial efficiency, on the one hand, and the public interest, on the other? What weight do they attach to profitability and what weight is given to various social objectives? Second, insofar as significant variations exist in the goal orientations of board members, are there any discernible organizational or role-related factors which account for these variations? In particular, do part-timers differ in their orientations from full-timers? Do those who have executive responsibilities differ from those who do not carry such responsibilities? Do board members appointed on a partisan basis exhibit different goal orientations from those appointed on an impartial basis? Third, is there any empirical evidence to support the contention that self-interest plays an important role in shaping the goal orientations of top-level management in public enterprise?

None of the methods usually employed in investigating the goal orientations of organizational leaders, seemed, in itself, sufficiently reliable and adequate for our investigation – mainly because they lean heavily on verbal statements without an attempt having been made to check the validity of these statements.

It was considered that an adaptation of the customary methods coupled with some specially designed cross-validation measures would be more adequate and reliable. This consideration proved to be fully justified as will become evident from the following survey of findings.

A widely used technique in the research of goal orientations is to ask the people involved to state the objectives of the organization as they perceive them. Following this method, board members were asked during the interview to state how they *personally* see the objectives of the corporation they are heading and, as a second step, to grade these objectives according to degree of importance. The results appear in Table 5.1.

Table 5.1   "Most important"[a] corporate objective(s) mentioned by board members (rounded-percentages)

Type of Objective	Britain	Israel
Making a profit	50	34
Supplying local demand	39	32
Producing a basic product (service)	22	25
Pace-maker in the industry	11	14
Saving/earning foreign exchange	6	21

[a] Board members were allowed to grade a the same degree of importance more than one objective which explains why the totals exceed 100.

As can be seen, profitability emerges as the most frequently mentioned first objective in both the Israeli and the British sample. In Britain, as compared to Israel, a higher percentage of board members, 50% as compared to 34%, mentioned profitability as the most important objective. However, the overall percentages conceal some important differences in attitude among the membership groups composing the boards.

A more detailed analysis of the data revealed that part-timers and full-timers, in both countries, differ greatly in their attitudes toward profitability. In the British sample about 83% of the full-timers gave first priority to profitability, whereas only a small percentage, about 16% of the part-timers did so. Similarly, in the Israeli sample only 29% of part-timers mentioned profitability as the most important objective while about 50% of full-timers did so. In other words, part-timers in both countries attach much less importance to the objective of profitability in comparison to full-timers.

The substitution of the profit objective with various social objectives is considered to be a source of the multiplicity of goals in public enterprise (e.g., Schneyer 1970; Davies 1963). Part-timers, as we have just shown, do not see profitability as the most important objective. Do they also tend to mention, on average, more objectives than the full-timers? Our data indicate that this is indeed so. Thus, in the British sample about 18% of full-timers mentioned three or more objectives, whereas 43% of part-timers did so. In the Israeli sample, about 33% of the full-timers mentioned four or more objectives, whereas about 50% of the part-timers did so.

Some reseachers maintain that statements about an organization's goals are often directed toward "external consumption" and do not reflect the "true" orientations of policy-makers (e.g., Etzioni 1964: 7; Perrow 1961).

It was felt therefore that more insight into the goal orientations of board members could be gained by investigating those value premises relating to some central issues of resource allocation. Two somewhat "provocative" questions were put before board members during the interview:

1. "Would you approve of an investment which is profitable to the corporation but not to the economy?" (Yes/No)
2. "Would you approve of an investment which is profitable to the economy but not to the corporation?" (Yes/No)

The results presented in Table 5.2 show, again, that full-timers differ significantly from part-timers in their attitudes toward profitability. Whereas 64% of full-timers in Israel and 92% of full-timers in Britain would approve of an investment which is profitable to the corporation but not to the economy, only 20% of part-timers in Israel and 50% of part-timers in Britain would do so.

Table 5.2   Basic premises in resource allocation decisions (rounded-percentages)

A. Approval of investment profitable to corporation but not to economy

		"Yes"	"No"	Total
Britain	full-timers	92	8	100
	part-timers	50	50	100
Israel	full-timers	64	36	100
	part-timers	20	80	100

B. Approval of investment profitable to economy but not to corporation

		"Yes"	"No"	Total
Britain	full-timers	20	80	100
	part-timers	66	34	100
Israel	full-timers	20	80	100
	part-timers	33	67	100

A reversal of attitudes takes place, however, among full-timers when the question is whether they would approve of an investment which is not profitable to the corporation, but is to the economy. About 80% of full-timers, in both samples, would not approve of such an investment. An interesting difference emerges between the British and the Israeli part-timers. Whereas two-thirds of the latter would not approve of such an investment, about the same proportion of the former would approve of it.

In Israel, as already mentioned, we had access to the detailed minutes of board discussions. We used these to further probe the question of goal orientations among board members. This was done by means of a content analysis of all the discussions relating to various topics of resource allocation, during the previous three years. The design of the content analysis was based on Simon's approach (1964) to the question of organizational goals and their measurement. According to Simon:

In decision-making situations of real life, a course of action, to be acceptable, must satisfy a whole set of requirements or constraints. Sometimes one of these requirements is singled out and referred to as the goal of action.

... For many purposes it is more meaningful to refer to the whole set of requirements as the (complex) goal of the action. This applies to both individual and organizational decision-making. First, the goals may be used directly to synthesize proposed solutions (alternative generation). Second, the goals may be used to test the satisfactoriness of a proposed solution (alternative testing) (1964: 4–5).

Contents were categorized into "constraints" and "goals." A "constraint" was defined as that content item which answers the question: "What (in the view of a certain person) should be taken into consideration in discussing a particular decision." According to this definition the category of constraints includes those considerations raised in the process of "alternative generation" and "alternative testing" in deciding upon a particular course of action.

For example, in one of the corporations studied, the question of upgrading the quality of its product arose after difficulties in marketing were encountered. Various technical methods were proposed ("alternative generation") and each of them was studied and discussed ("alternative testing") taking into consideration various constraints, such as technical feasibility, the cost of investments, profitability of the proposed method, the quality of the final product, etc. These considerations comprised the list of constraints relating to the above subject.

A "goal" was defined as that content item which explicitly mentioned a "desirable state of affairs" as an object of positive aspiration, thus differentiating between those states of affairs which are *positively* desired and those which are merely acceptable (the statements may be phrased in different ways, e.g., "it is desired that," "our purpose is," "we ought to aim at," "our objective is" etc.

For example, in one of the corporations studied the management proposed a substantial investment in a new plant. The main argument put forth by the management was that without the proposed investment the company would have to close down. "Survival" was recorded as one of the goals mentioned in relation to that issue. Other goals recorded in relation to that issue were profitability to the company, profitability to the econ-omy, and so forth – which were mentioned by the board members as desiderata when the issue was raised.

A technical description of the content analysis is given in Appendix D. The final result of this analysis was a list of action goals and a list of constraints. These were then divided into a number of categories such as goals/constraints relating to the national economy or of a sociopolitical nature; those relating to financial or commercial aspects; or, those relating to the well-being of of the corporation.

Table 5.3 shows the frequencies of action goals mentioned by board members.

Table 5.3 "Action goals" mentioned by board members during board discus-sions on various issues of resource allocation (Israel) (percentages)

Type of Goal	Membership category			
	Full-timers	Part-timers	Chairmen	Total (*n*)
National economy; sociopolitical; political	6.7	50.0	39.5	(36)
Commercial; financial	26.7	19.0	39.5	(27)
Preservation of corpora-tion's status, independence and strength	66.6	31.0	21.0	(31)
Total (number of content items)	100.0 (15)	100.0 (41)	100.0 (38)	100.0 (94)

$\chi_4^2 = 16.06$ $0.01 \leq P \leq 0.02$

As can be seen, the majority (50%) of part-timers (chairmen excluded) emphasized sociopolitical objectives and objectives relating to the na-tional economy. In contrast, the majority (66%) of full-timers emphasized objectives relating to the well-being of the corporation, its status, inde-pendence, and strength. Commercial, financial, and economic efficiency objectives are second in importance as far as full-timers are concerned, whereas they are least important as far as part-timers are concerned.

It is interesting to note that chairmen attached equal importance to commercial, financial, and economic efficiency objectives, on the one hand, and to sociopolitical objectives and objectives relating to the national economy, on the other. In their attitudes they occupy a middle position between part-timers who are most concerned with various objectives of public interest and full-timers who are mainly concerned with the well-being of the corporation.

The data on "constraints" shown in Table 5.4 reveal some further matters of interest.

Table 5.4   "Constraints" mentioned by board members during board discussions on various issues of resource allocation (Israel) (percentages)

Type of Goal	Membership category			
	Full-timers	Part-timers	Chairmen	Total (*n*)
National economy; sociopolitical; political	9.4	44.0	33.7	(97)
Commercial; financial	63.3	45.3	48.3	(146)
Preservation of corporation's status, independence, and strength	27.3	10.7	19.0	(50)
Total (number of content items)	100.0 (58)	100.0 (140)	100.0 (95)	100.0 (293)

$\chi_4^2 = 30.74$ $P \le 0.001$

An important finding is that economic considerations are highly emphasized by all board members in deciding on various issues of resource allocation. The data also confirm our other findings showing that full-timers attach higher importance to economic considerations than do part-timers with the chairmen occupying a middle position. Whereas considerations relating to the national economy and to various sociopolitical matters are second in importance as far as the part-timers and the chairmen are concerned, such considerations are far behind considerations relating to the well-being of the corporation, as far as full-timers are concerned. The content analysis not only confirmed our findings based on the interviews, but also revealed some new aspects about the goal orientations of board members: First, that the well-being of the corporation is an important objective of full-timers, and occupies an important place in their considerations relating to matters of resource allocation. Second, that board chairmen tend to have attitudes intermediate to those of full-timers, on the one hand, and part-timers, on the other. We will return to these findings when evaluating all our findings against certain broader theoretical theses.

It is perhaps important to note that the board members themselves, in Israel as well as in Britain, are well aware of these differences in attitude between full-timers and part-timers towards profitability, on the one hand, and social objectives, on the other.

Let us cite some of the part-timers[1]:

I accept the statutory duty that... [name of corporation] provides a national service and does it efficiently. Social objectives equal and reinforce the commercial purposes. Some full-time board members may put more emphasis on profit (B 1–3).

I express my point of view. It may be different from the views of others... from the views of full-time board members. We are nationalized industry. Therefore if government demands certain things (like keeping prices down) we ought to meet these demands. ...On the other hand, the people managing the corporation want a completely commercial enterprise to run for reasons of management (B 4–2).

Citing some of the full-timers:

It is possible that some part-time board members would put profitability after various socioeconomic objectives in order of importance (I 26–357).

For me, the commercial success of the corporation is more important than to part-time board members. [They] ... tend to emphasize social objectives. For example, the board [composed of part-timers mostly, M.D.] prevented us from hiring some equipment at very profitable terms; in their opinion the corporation exists only in order to be of service to the country (I 25–122).

I see myself as the sole custodian of the economic objectives (I 11–136).

Perhaps the ultimate test of the importance attached by board members to profitability as against other social objectives is whether they see in it, or not, the raison d'être of the corporation. The following question was intended to test this issue:

Is the existence of this corporation justified:
(a) without being profitable (Yes/No)?
(b) without being profitable to the economy (Yes/No)?

The results are presented in Table 5.5.

When the responses to both questions are considered simultaneously, board members in both samples emerge as about equally divided between the view that profitability – to the corporation or to the economy – is an essential justification for the existence of the corporation, and the view that its existence might well be justified on other grounds. A detailed

Table 5.5   Responses concerning the justification of corporate existence
(rounded percentages)

	Without profitability			Without profitability to economy		
	"Yes"	"No"	Total	"Yes"	"No"	Total
Britain	63	37	100	53	47	100
Israel	49	51	100	36	64	100

analysis of the responses to each question revealed that the above division
of views applies more or less also when part-timers and full-timers are
considered separately. This finding raises the following questions: If full-
timers do not see in profitability the raison d'être of the corporation more
than do part-timers, what is the explanation for the significantly higher
emphasis they put (in comparison to part-timers) on profitability as an
objective, and as a criterion for resource allocation? To answer this question we must turn from bare statistics to an analysis of statements made by
full-timers when discussing the objectives of the corporation. A number of
themes recurred in these statements, as follows:

1. Profit provides management with clear decision-making criteria:

I would not forego the objective of profit because one loses a clear standard. I
have doubts whether other objectives could be established. If you abolish the
commercial principle – who is going to judge what is good and what is bad (B 2–3)?

Profit is a yardstick; a measure of the community's willingness to pay for the
services provided (B 3–1).

2. Profit is an essential measure of managerial efficiency:

One must have a profit motive because otherwise how will you measure efficiency?

3. Profit ensures the corporation's continued (untroubled) existence:

This is not a social business. It is a commercial undertaking. Existence means to
make a profit. You don't make a profit and your existence is in danger (B 2–3).

Our objective is to accumulate funds for future investments. As soon as you are
large enough you must secure funds for future existence; make as large profits as
you can, provided that the service you give is at a standard at which complaints
from the public [the users of the service, M.D.] are at minimum. Have enough
finance, well enough in advance of the time you'll need it. Try and secure freedom
from the consequences of economic fluctuations (B 2–6).

Of course... we have to pay attention to social matters... but at the same time make a profit. A profit which will enable us to make a proper allowance for finance in future (B 3–3).

Profit is the primary objective. One should see to it that the other objectives... should not interfere with it. Otherwise the existence of the corporation is in danger (I 21–157).

4. Profit provides the means for corporate growth and expansion:

[T]o break even, but not only; to build up adequate reserves (bearing in mind social implications and customer service).

Reserves build-up is really to achieve a situation where a fair proportion of expansion can be achieved. We want complete independence at self-financing and expansion (B 3–4).

Management must see before its eyes the main objective which is profit... We must earn a profit and grow... (I 17–337).

5. Profit serves as a safeguard of managerial autonomy vis-à-vis government:

[T]here is great motivation to break even because if we get in trouble government poke their noses into our business.

...Profit enables the company to be autonomous. But there is a danger in too much profit. This is also an occasion for interference (B 2–5).

If you are earning sufficient money you can carry out your plans. You are in a much better position to impose your will (B 2–3).

There is a great deal of difference if you have enough money and don't need to resort to government financing; you are free to do what you wish (B 2–6).

We do not strive to maximum profit but we want to achieve a good profit. It is not healthy to have very high profits. High profits call for interference... I see a challenge in self-financing and self-management. As long as we do not need money we have freedom. We keep our accounts 'conservatively' – in order to accumulate reserves. If we didn't we would show too high profits in certain years; this would lead, ultimately, to a contraction in accumulated reserves (I 11–136).

Many full-timers expressed the view that the main task of management is to "maintain the viability of the corporation." When asked what they meant by viability the answers usually took on the form of statements similar to those under (3) and (4) above. From the above it follows that profitability is perceived by those in charge of the daily management of the corporation as a means to a variety of ends, the most important of which are: a yardstick for managerial decision-making and managerial performance, the continued existence and growth of the corporation, and managerial autonomy.

62

Summary. Our findings indicate that the attitudes of board members toward the two principal norms supposed to guide the conduct of public enterprise, economic efficiency and the public interest, are quite complex. On the whole we found that profitability occupies an important place in the goal orientations of all board members. Yet the importance attached to it does not carry equal weight in relation to all issues involved and in relation to all board members. Thus, insofar as the raison d'être of the corporation is concerned, board members, full timers and part-timers alike, are divided in their views as to whether profitability should, or should not, be the decisive criterion.

On the other hand, considerations of economic efficiency and profitability were found to far outweigh all other considerations when resource allocation decisions are at stake; this applies to full-timers and part-timers alike. However, the former attach considerably more importance to such considerations than do the latter. In addition, full-timers were found to emphasize much more than part-timers profitability as a desirable objective which the corporation should strive to achieve. In contrast, part-timers tend to attach more importance to various social and national objectives.

The well-being of the corporation, its status, growth, and its continued existence, were found to be of very high importance to full-timers. Profitability is perceived by them as an important means toward the attainment of these ends. Profitability is also perceived by them as a means for maintaining managerial autonomy and managerial independence from government interference, and as a yardstick for managerial decision-making and managerial performance.

Notes

[1] The letters in parentheses at the end of the citations mean: "B" – Britain; "I" – Israel; the numbers identify the company and the person.

Chapter Six
Board Members' Attitudes Toward Governmental Control

Government control, as many illustrations in the literature show, is often a source of conflictual relationships between those representing the government and those representing the public enterprise. The overall impression is that the majority of conflicts arise because the legitimacy of governmental authority over various matters concerning the conduct of the enterprise is often questioned and contested by those heading the public enterprise. It is however difficult, because of the particularistic nature of the cases cited, to arrive at definite conclusions as to the specific causes of the problem.

Given the fact that the purposes of governmental control as well as the potential points of governmental intervention in the affairs of the corporation are manifold, a more systematic approach is needed to investigate the issues at stake. The aims of our investigation were to locate the major problem areas through a systematic inquiry into the attitudes of board members toward the various facets of governmental control, to find out to what extent board members are willing to accept constraints on the freedom of the corporation stemming from the pursuit, by government, of various socioeconomic and political objectives, and in particular, to reveal what spheres of corporate activity are perceived by board members as legitimate points of governmental intervention and what spheres should be excluded, in their opinion, from such intervention.

A second line of investigation is related to another allegedly problematic fact of governmental control in public enterprise, namely, the widespread contention among those concerned with the conduct of the public enterprise, that governmental control – even when it is not a source of conflictual relationships – is detrimental to managerial initiative and to managerial morale. An attempt was made to examine whether, and to what extent, this contention is indeed sustained by empirical evidence.

There are two major interrelated contexts in which the problem of governmental control in public enterprise arises. One concerns the use of the corporation as a tool for implementing various economic and sociopolitical policies (notably the maintenance of full employment, the control of inflation, and the promotion of economic growth). The other concerns long-term corporate planning. Our investigation regarding the attitudes of board members toward governmental control concentrated on the key issues in these two areas.

One such key issue is the use of public enterprise for the implementation of short- and long-term national economic policy. The following question concerning short-term national economic policy was put to the board members during the interview:

In your opinion, should this corporation serve as a means for implementing government policy in the following spheres: employment/wages/prices/investments. (Yes/No – regarding each of the spheres)

In both samples, the British and the Israeli, the majority of board members (about two-thirds) replied "No." In general, the reply patterns of part-timers and full-timers did not differ significantly.

In the Israeli sample, though, the percentage of full-timers who replied "No" was a bit higher than the percentage of part-timers who did so, but the differences are not statistically significant. When encouraged to elaborate on the subject, most full-timers expressed their view against using the corporation for implementing short-term economic policies. A recurrent comment was that "politicians are shortsighted," that they have "a short-term horizon," and should therefore be prevented from interfering with the corporation's affairs insofar as *current* economic policies are concerned. However, there was some willingness to comply with government policy if applied *universally* to all, public and private enterprise alike. Some representative statements:

I am against using nationalized industries as a means for implementing short-term government policies. . . .

I am for control through planning. . . . Also we should comply with overall government policy. . . . I am against intervention for purely short-term political reasons and social reasons because politicians have a short-term horizon (B 3–1).

A corporation is not a political organ but a commercial undertaking. It should not be used therefore as a means for implementing current government policy (I 25–35).

This corporation was established to supply a service and not as a tool for government policy (I 22–344).

Many full-timers complained specifically about government interference in regard to prices and wages. They expressed resentment against the influence this has on the thinking of board members.

The most profound effect is on people's thoughts. Board members ask themselves 'how will government react to this?' Especially when we are dealing with wage claims, we get very closely involved with government (B 5–2).

In pricing policy we are very much concerned with the ideas of government about pricing; we are influenced by these ideas (B 3–4).

A somewhat different attitude was displayed by many part-timers. They were somewhat less categoric in taking a stand. The following statements best reflect their attitudes, on average:

[W]e must approve constraints from shareholders; but government should be put into a position when it has to balance its interests against a very strong, fighting board which insists on government making its demands very explicitly and give full respect to the board (B 1–3).

I favor the constraints imposed by government on the corporation. The corporation should be guided by such considerations [i.e., serve as a means for implementing government policy, M.D.] since it is financed by government. But I would prefer that the corporation be given more latitude to exercise its considerations (B 4–2).

Clear principles should be established as to the legitimate sphere of influence of government. Government intervention should not be exercised ad hoc (I 20–263).

I am willing to cooperate but on the condition that the corporation be given the possibility to consider things ad hoc and decide in each case (I 18–282).

It is recurrently argued in the literature that the ill-feelings against ad hoc governmental intervention could be greatly alleviated if government agreed to compensate or subsidize the corporation for imposing constraints on its freedom to act according to commercial considerations. How far is this assumption true? We asked board members to express their views on subsidies and financial aid. Full-timers and part-timers alike, in both samples, were generally against subsidies "on a permanent basis." However, most of the part-timers favored subsidies if needed for social reasons. Full-timers, on the other hand, maintained that subsidies create dependency on government and bring about unwanted governmental interference; they are also a disincentive to management and undermine managerial efficiency. Therefore, if absolutely necessary, subsidies should be given directly to the corporation's suppliers or to its customers. Some representative statements of part-timers:

I wouldn't favor subsidies as normal. But if needed for social reasons, or to cover uncommercial operations which we are required to undertake – yes (B 4–2).

I think we should be strong enough to take subsidies. If government wants certain services to be provided which need subsidizing we should be prepared to take them for the good of the nation (B 1–3).

It is wrong to have subsidies on a national scale. On the other hand, where necessary to meet social demands, government subsidies should be accepted (B 2–2).

Some representative statements of full-timers:

I do not favor subsidies because they mean intervention (B 1–1).

I am generally not in favor of subsidies. ...we were subsidized when we were forced to practice price restraint. The subsidizing was aimed at break-even only. We could have been much more profitable if we could practice commercial pricing (B 3–4).

I was, and am, against these [subsidies, M. D.] because it really does not improve the economic actions of the company. If government wants it should subsidize the suppliers (B 1–5).

In general I am against subsidies; they are a very inefficient way of running a business. Government has vastly overdone subsidizing for short-term political reasons (B 3–3).

Writing off – this is bad, because it destroys initiative (B 2–3).

When asked to "comment, generally on government interference," full-timers and part-timers emerged as having very similar attitudes: both complained, quite equally, about too much interference.
Part-timers:

The corporation suffers much from a continuous rigging, continuous surveillance (B 4–1).

You have their [minister's/officials', M. D.] *nagging*. You have no freedom to act on trust. So you have this difficult environment. You have to divide yourself between running the business and dealing with the government (B 1–3).

Full-timers:

Having to ask all the time 'my dad' is not a very good way of operations (B 3–1).

The day-to-day crawling over many details by government is unnecessary. The cost involved is huge and unnecessary... to keep them up to date on a daily basis; to be ready to answer all the questions off-the-cuff. Whitehall has to be informed, and I was one of the bridge builders – but the complexity and detail of the whole thing has grown to dimensions impossible (B 5–1).

Many board members thought that interference varies considerably with the financial position of the corporation:

Interference comes when the minister is exposed to losses. . . in times when doing well – we don't have much interference so that the intensity of interference varies (B 1–2).

The major factor in intervention is the financial position of the corporation; there is less intervention when successful (B 5–3).

The only solution to avoid interference seems to be to earn enough money to keep yourself in business (B 2–3).
In general, if you are making a profit you are much less prone to interference. What gets them really off your back is the ability to pay a dividend. This is the key (B 4–2).

When the question was raised – what, specifically, are the dysfunctions of government interference in the current affairs of the corporation, replies centered around two topics. Some board members emphasized that such interference impairs the ability of the corporation to react expediently to opportunities and market forces. Others, maintained that such controls sometimes obstruct and cause severe distortions in the implementation of long-term corporate plans, and have therefore a negative impact on the corporation's economic efficiency.

Views differ, however, in relation to long-term corporate planning. There was general agreement that government *should* play a major role insofar as the overall long-term policy of the corporation is concerned. It was considered by many that reaching an agreement with government about policy, would lead to a more peaceful relationship, and less intervention in the daily affairs of the corporation.

One appreciates that politicians even if intelligent people, inevitably take a series of short-term views, and this could be disastrous. Therefore, we see it as part of our job to continuously take long-term views. We invest much time in this. But, we also should realize that there is no point in arguing about the short-term views of politicians. Rather, the aim should be to work out a particular relationship with government (B 3–3).

Indeed, board members in one of the corporations which acted according to a corporate plan, agreed upon with government years ago, stated quite clearly that "luckily" their corporation did not experience much intervention. Constraints imposed on prices – yes; but not intervention in the daily affairs of the corporation. Board members in another corporation which came to an agreement with government on a long-term corporate plan close to the time of our research, expressed the hope that this agreement will lead to less intervention in the daily affairs of the corporation.

Does the frequent governmental intervention in the affairs of the corporation create a feeling, among board members, of powerlessness? Is it a disincentive to managerial initiative? A somewhat provocative question was put before full-time board members. They were asked whether there is a feeling among management "that after all, the corporation will have its way?" The majority answered with an unqualified "Yes." Some qualified their positive replies by stating that "not always" would the corporation be able to have its way.

The accompanying rationales for the feeling of powerfulness were usually of two kinds. Some emphasized the importance of the product/service provided by the corporation:

Yes, we think that our services are necessary. Therefore our existence will have to continue, and if so, we've got to have what we need (B 2–6).

Some emphasized the constraints of a competitive environment:

Government tried sometimes to impose national interests, but we do not take them very seriously, because we are operating in a very competitive environment, and we have to adapt to that environment.... Decisions may be *modified* by government policy.... But on the whole I would say 'no' to the question whether we feel very constrained by government pressures (B 1–5).

Another index of confidence in its own power is the readiness of management to engage in "risky" decisions, i.e., decisions for which government approval was needed but was not yet given. All deputy chairmen admitted that from time to time the corporation has taken, and has proceeded with the implementation of such decisions. It was generally admitted that management had to engage, willy-nilly, in "politics" in order to have its way:

You have to have a good political instinct because really you make political decisions. For example, when you employ various political strategies to have your way. But I don't like it. One likes to have a well-defined situation, and not deal constantly with political manoeuvring (B 5–2).

This longing for a "well-defined situation," and the general dislike of and frustration from having to engage in politics was a recurrent theme mainly with those at the apex of the executive pyramid who, obviously, are engaged most heavily in the political game.

Perhaps the most revealing indicator of management's relative strength is the weight board members attach to the executive management, on the one hand, and to government, on the other, in determining the objectives of the corporation. In both samples, the British and the Israeli, about 70% of the board members believed that the executive management determines to a very high degree the objectives of the corporation. In comparison, only 18% of board members in the British sample and 47% in the

Israeli sample attached similar importance to the minister. It is worthwhile noting that though board members in Israel did not differ from their British counterparts in the degree of importance attributed to the executive management in determining the objectives of the corporation, a much higher proportion than in Britain thought that the minister, too, plays a major role in this process. We will return later on to comment on this finding.

The general picture which emerges from the various indices discussed is that the executive management of the corporation in both settings, the Israeli and the British, feels itself quite powerful vis-à-vis government – in spite of their complaints against governmental interference in the affairs of the corporation.

Summary. It is evident that board members differentiate quite sharply between two types of governmental controls. While they fully accept the legitimacy of governmental authority and are willing to comply with the objectives and guidelines set by government, they take a negative view toward ad-hoc controls and intervention in the current affairs of the corporation. The latter are believed to be guided by narrow, short-term political considerations and interests, and are therefore viewed as far less legitimate. Moreover, ad-hoc controls and interventions in the current affairs of the corporation are resented since it is felt that they impair the corporation's capability to react expediently to market forces. They are also viewed as an obstacle in the implementation of long-term corporate plans.

It is interesting to note that there exists a widespread belief, especially among full-timers, that an agreement with government about the basic objectives of the corporation and about its long-term policy could serve as a safeguard against ad-hoc governmental intervention and controls. Paradoxically, therefore, resentment of ad-hoc governmental intervention is accompanied by a willingness to accept governmental control and guidance insofar as this results in an agreed upon framework for the long-term conduct of the corporation. Another point of emphasis is that the attitudes toward governmental controls are not quite identical insofar as full- and part-time board members are concerned. Though differences are not as salient as with regard to goal orientations, some interesting nuances are revealed. Part-timers tend to agree to ad-hoc governmental controls provided that such controls are necessary for the implementation of current economic policy, and if the corporation is "adequately" compensated for the restraints imposed on it. On the other hand, full-timers tend to take a negative attitude toward such controls even if compensation is assured.

Subsidies are shunned since it is believed that they are, unavoidably, accompanied by greater government interference; that they provide only partial compensation for the restraints imposed on the corporation; and that they are bad for the morale of the corporation, among others, because they remove the profit incentive.

There is a strong belief among all board members that financial self-sufficiency is an efficient safeguard against government intervention. Consequently, there exists a strong drive especially among full-timers to achieve such self-sufficiency.

Notwithstanding the fact that government controls are believed to far surpass the desired, the executive management does not feel powerless at all vis-à-vis government. On the contrary, it feels, on the whole, quite strong and able to achieve, this way or the other, what it wills. Of special significance is perhaps the general belief among board members that the corporate management plays a most important role in shaping the objectives of the corporation.

Chapter Seven
Board Members' Perceptions of the Functions of the Board

The analysis of role perceptions focused on the following major questions. First, what are the conceptions of the board members concerning the functions of the board and to what extent is there agreement on this issue? Second, how far do the actual workings of the board match the expectations of board members? Third, what are the expectations of the various membership groups within the board concerning their specific roles on the board, and how far are these expectations fulfilled in practice?

When confronted with a general question about the functions of the board, all board members, in Israel as well as in Britain, agreed that the major function of the board is policy-making. Policy-making is, however, a rather vague concept which does not disclose very much about the conceptions of board members concerning the specific policy-making functions of the board. To obtain a more accurate picture about these, board members were questioned about their views concerning the allocation of decision-making powers between government, the board, and the executive management.

Our interview included the following questions:

1. "Who should have the authority to decide on the following matters . . .?"
2. "Who should have the authority to finally approve the following matters . . .?" (The authority of approval was defined as final, and above the authority of decision.)

Both questions were followed by a list of major decision issues on resource allocation and current policy as follows:

Resource Allocation
- Total investment
- Type of production lines
- Investment in production lines
- R & D investments
- Timing of investments

Current Policy
- Production policy
- Pricing policy
- Employment and wages policy
- Procurement policy

Board members were asked to indicate, in relation to each decision issue, which is the most desirable locus of decision: the executive management, the board of directors, or the government (the minister and other government representatives).

In Britain, response patterns were quite stereotypic: the board members seemed reluctant to digress in their responses from the statutory allocation of decision-making powers. The interviewer had the feeling that the interviewees refrained from a free expression of their opinion since the digression may be interpreted as a deliquent or rebellious attitude toward the statutes. We decided therefore to discontinue these questions in the British research.

The results reported below are, therefore, based exclusively on the Israeli sample. Since at the time of the research in Israel no statutory, or any other formal provisions existed regarding the allocation of decision-making powers, response patterns would probably be unbiased in this respect.

What immediately becomes apparent from Table 7.1 is that, in general,

Table 7.1 Perceptions regarding appropriate loci of decision (Israel) (percentages)

Appropriate Locus of Decision / Type of Decision	Executive Management		Board of Directors and Management[a]		Board of Directors		Board of Directors and Government		Government and its Representatives		Total
Total investment	28.6		14.3		57.1		0.0		0.0		100 (14)
		11.6		4.7		72.1		0.0		11.6	100 (43)
Type of production lines	78.6		7.1		14.3		0.0		0.0		100 (14)
		47.6		4.8		47.6		0.0		0.0	100 (42)
Production policy	100.0		0.0		0.0		0.0		0.0		100 (14)
		78.6		2.4		19,0		0.0		11.6	100 (42)
Type/level of investment in production lines	64.3		14.3		21.4		0.0		0.0		100 (14)
		52.4		11.9		35.7		0.0		0.0	100 (42)
R & D investments	69.2		15.4		15.4		0.0		0.0		100 (13)
		39.5		16.3		44.2		0.0		0.0	100 (43)
Timing of investments	85.7		7.1		7.2		0.0		0.0		100 (14)
		62.8		4.7		30.2		2.3		0.0	100 (43)
Pricing policy investments	78.6		7.1		14.3		0.0		0.0		100 (14)
		53.5		4.7		37.2		2.3		2.3	100 (43)
Employment policy	100.0		0.0		0.0		0.0		0.0		100 (14)
		55.8		9.3		34.9		0.0		0.0	100 (43)
Procurement policy	100.0		0.0		0.0		0.0		0.0		100 (14)
		90.7		4.7		4.6		0.0		0.0	100 (43)

[a] This category was not mentioned by interviewer but was proposed by some of those interviewed. Upper left, full-timers; lower right, part-timers; numbers in parentheses, number of respondents

part-timers and full-timers diverge quite sharply in their attitudes. There are only a few exceptions to this generalization. Thus, both groups display similar attitudes in relation to the locus of *decision* on "total investment" on "investment in production lines," and on "procurement policy."

In relation to the locus of *approval* there is again a similarity in attitudes on "total investment" and on "investment in production lines" (Table 7.2).

Table 7.2 Perceptions regarding appropriate loci of approval (Israel) (percentages)

Appropriate Locus of Decision / Type of Decision	Executive Management	Board of Directors and Management[a]	Board of Directors	Board of Directors and Government	Government and its Representatives	Total
Total investment	0.0	0.0	50.0	14.3	35.7	100 (14)
	0.0	0.0	39.5	7.9	52.6	100 (38)
Type of production lines	50.0	0.0	42.9	7.1	0.0	100 (14)
	8.8	0.0	82.4	2.9	5.9	100 (34)
Production policy	64.3	7.1	28.6	0.0	0.0	100 (14)
	35.3	2.9	61.8	0.0	0.0	100 (34)
Type/level of investment in production lines	14.3	0.0	78.6	7.1	0.0	100 (14)
	7.7	2.6	82.1	0.0	7.6	100 (39)
R & D investments	73.1	0.0	26.9	0.0	0.0	100 (13)
	10.6	5.3	78.9	2.6	2.6	100 (38)
Timing of investments	7.1	7.1	85.8	0.0	0.0	100 (14)
	25.0	2.8	55.6	2.8	13.8	100 (33)
Pricing policy	71.4	0.0	21.4	0.0	7.2	100 (14)
	21.1	0.0	65.8	0.0	13.1	100 (38)
Employment policy	64.3	0.0	35.7	0.0	0.0	100 (14)
	20.0	5.7	65.7	2.9	5.7	100 (35)
Procurement policy	85.7	0.0	14.3	0.0	0.0	100 (14)
	54.5	3.0	39.4	0.0	3.1	100 (33)

[a] This category was not mentioned by interviewer but was proposed by some of those interviewed. Upper left, full-timers; lower right, part-timers; numbers in parentheses, number of respondents.

In relation to all decision issues, apart from "total investment" the majority, two-thirds and more, of the full-timers expressed the belief that decisions should be in the hands of the executive management. Part-timers, however, are divided between the board and the executive management, in relation to most issues.

As far as the locus of approval is concerned, the picture is much more variegated. The majority of full-timers believe that approvals on "total investments," "investments in production lines," and on "timing of investments" should be in the hands of the board, whereas "R & D investments," "pricing policy," "employment and wages policy," "production policy," and "procurement policy" should be left in the hands of the executive management. In contrast, the majority of part-timers would not leave the approval on any of the issues, with the exception of "procurement policy", in the hands of the executive management. Rather, they believe that approvals should be in the hands of the board.

It is interesting to note that in relation to one decision issue only, "total

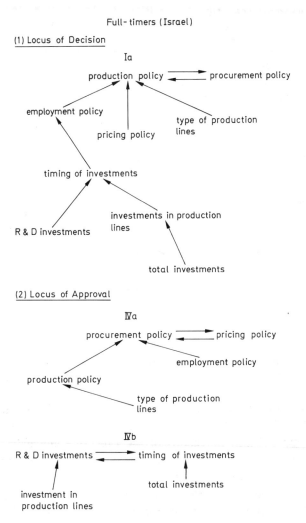

Figure 7.1   Results of cluster analysis on responses regarding the appropriate loci of decision and approval

investment," do we find a substantial percentage (about 50%) of board members from among both groups, full-timers and part-timers, who believe that approval should be in the hands of the government.

The above differences between part-timers and full-timers stand out more sharply and become more meaningful when the results of a clustering method (see Appendix E) which was applied to the data are displayed (Figs. 7.1 and 7.2).

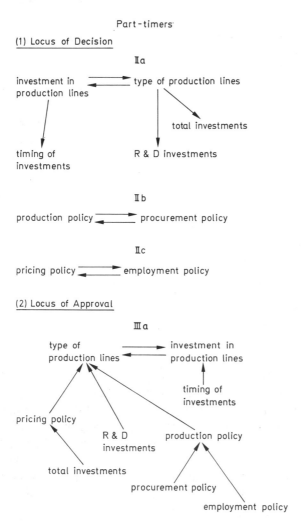

Figure 7.2   Results of cluster analysis on responses regarding the appropriate loci of decision and approval

Let us start with an analysis of the clusters obtained concerning the *locus of decision*. The single cluster containing all decision issues (Ia), indicates that full-timers tend to regard all these issues as belonging to one "universe," and reflects their attitude that the appropriate locus of decision for these issues is the executive management. In contrast, the three clusters (IIa), (IIb), and (IIc), indicate that part-timers tend to differentiate between the various issues as belonging to different universes. Table 7.3 displays the frequencies of responses according to cluster.

Table 7.3 Part-timers' responses according to type of cluster and appropriate locus of decision (Israel) (percentages)

Cluster	Locus of Decision				
	Executive Management	Executive Management and Board	Board	Government and its Representatives	Total
IIa (Investments)	43.0	9.2	46.0	1.8	100.0
IIc (Employment/ Pricing)	55.0	7.1	36.5	1.4	100.0
IIb (Procurement/ Production Policy)	85.0	3.2	11.8	0.0	100.0
$\chi^2 = 44.2$ $P \leq .001$					

While on average about 85% of part-timers believe that the appropriate locus of decision on procurement and production policies is the executive management, only 55% on average, believe that this is also the appropriate locus of decision on employment and pricing policies; only 43%, on average, believe that various investment issues should be decided by the executive management.

The differences between full-timers and part-timers in regard to two of the clusters (IIa and IIc) were found to be statistically significant. (See Appendix F for the detailed comparison.)

In regard to the *locus of approval* the picture is reversed. The single cluster (IIIa) containing all decision issues, indicates that part-timers tend to regard all these issues as belonging to one universe and reflects their attitude that the appropriate locus of approval for these issues is the board of directors. On the other hand, clusters (IVa) and (IVb) indicate that full-timers tend to differentiate between decision issues relating to invest-ments and decision issues relating to aspects of current policy. Table 7.4 displaying the full-timers' frequencies of responses in regard to the various clusters shows that close to two-thirds of them view the board as the appropriate locus of approval for investments. Yet, in regard to current policy matters the executive management is perceived as the appropriate locus of approval by more than two-thirds of the full-timers.

Table 7.4 Full-timers' responses according to type of cluster and appropriate locus of approval (Israel) (percentages)

| Cluster | Locus of Decision | | | | |
	Executive Manage- ment	Executive Manage- ment and Board	Board	Govern- ment and its Repre- sentatives	Total
IVa (current policy)	67.0	1.6	28.5	2.9	100.0
IVb (investments)	23.5	1.8	60.0	14.7	100.0
$\chi^2 = 31.90$ $P \leq 0.001$					

The differences between full-timers and part-timers were found to be significant in relation to cluster IVa. (See Appendix G for the detailed comparison.)

So much for a detailed description of findings. They may be summa-rized as follows. Though there is general agreement among board mem-bers that the board should function mainly as a policy-making body, part-timers and full-timers diverge in their views as to exactly what policy-making powers should be entrusted to the board. Full-timers tend to believe that the board should function mainly as a body entrusted with the power to approve decisions made at the executive level. They also believe that decisions on matters of current policy should not be subjected at all to the approval of the board.

Full-timers do not tend, in general, to regard the board as the appropriate place for arriving at major long-term and short-term policy decisions. Rather, they believe that the appropriate locus where these decisions should be arrived at is the executive management. In contrast, a substantial proportion of part-timers believe that decisions related to investments, and decisions on pricing policy and employment policy should be reached at the board level.

Full-timers and part-timers also differ in their views about what decisions should be approved at the board level. Whereas part-timers tend to believe that all decisions should be approved at that level, full-timers tend to believe that decisions on matters of current policy (production, pricing, employment, and personnel) should not be subject to the approval of the board.

It seems that the attitudes of full-timers and part-timers are based on the following major considerations. First, there is the recognition that decision-making is an intricate, complex, and time-consuming process, which necessitates above all expertise and close knowledge of the material. Both, full-timers and part-timers alike, seem to agree that in this respect the board, composed partly of part-timers, is not the most suitable decision-making forum. To cite a few examples:

In practice, part-timers do not contribute much to decisions because of the complexity of matters involved and the technical knowledge needed (Deputy chairman, full-time).

Most part-time board members do not have the detailed knowledge necessary, and their participation in decision making is only symbolic (Part-timer).

Part-timers lack expertise, time and information. They cannot engage effectively in policy-making (Part-timer).

However, it seems that insofar as part-timers are concerned, the above consideration is often overridden by the reluctance to leave important decisions, i. e., decisions related in some way to the public interest, in the hands of the executive management. This would explain why a substantial proportion of part-timers insists that decisions related to investments, which have, naturally, important implications for the future of the corporation, and for the objectives pursued by it, should be made at the board level. This would also explain the differentiation, by part-timers, between pricing and employment policy, on the one hand, and procurement and production policy, on the other. The first may have important implications for current national economic policy, which would explain why a substantial proportion of part-timers thought that they should be decided by the board. By the same token, production and procurement policy, obviously, are mostly of little consequence to current national economic policy, which would explain why the majority of part-timers would leave them to the executive management.

A third consideration is commercial flexibility. It seems that this consideration affects mainly the attitudes of full-timers and explains the differentiation they make between issues related to investments, on the one hand, and all current policy matters, on the other. While they agree that the first should be brought to the board for approval, they do not think so in relation to the latter. It seems that full-timers who have executive responsibilities wish to preserve maximum managerial autonomy in regard to these matters which greatly affect the commercial flexibility of the corporation and its capability to respond expediently and adequately to market forces. On the other hand, part-timers who do not feel the burden of daily management, but are concerned with the responsibilities of the board vis-à-vis government, and "the public at large," are reluctant to give full autonomy on these matters to the executive management.

So far for the views of board members concerning the *desired* allocation of decision-making powers and the share of the board in it. What is the situation in practice? What place does the board actually have in the decision-making process? When confronted with these questions the great majority of board members, about 80%, in Britain as well as in Israel expressed the view that the board functions mainly as a policy-approving body. About 50% thought that the board fulfills also some policy-making functions, especially in regard to major investments, pricing, and wages policies.

There was general agreement that the initiative on major policy issues comes only very rarely from the board and that it is mainly the executive management which initiates decisions. More precisely, executive management presents to the board specific and well-defined proposals for approval and the board merely reacts to this initiative. Sometimes, the original proposals are *modified* after discussions on the board.

How much influence on the affairs of the corporation is the board perceived to have in comparison to the executive management, to the government, and to other groups? Board members were asked to indicate who determines the objectives of the corporation and to what extent. The results are presented in Table 7.5.

In congruence with the findings discussed above, the executive management, and above all the chief executive officer emerge as the most influential, followed by the board.

Table 7.5   Perceived influence patterns in determining corporate objectives
              (rounded percentages)

	Influence					
	Very much		Quite a lot		A little bit	
	Br	Is	Br	Is	Br	Is
Chief Executive	69	60	13	33	–	–
Executive Management	56	17	6	45	–	–
Board of Directors	31	19	38	40	19	–
Minister Responsible	13	19	5	36	31	45
Minister of Finance	6	14	13	30	18	36
Government Officials	6	26	13	44	10	–
Employees	–	–	5	–	32	–
Consumers	5	–	5	–	30	–
Public at Large	–	–	–	–	18	–

Br, Britain; Is, Israel

In Israel, the board as a whole is considered less powerful than in Britain. However, a detailed analysis of the Israeli data reveals that part-timers tend to consider government representatives on the board as quite powerful: about 80% thought that government officials on the board have much influence over the corporation's objectives. In contrast, only about 30% of the full-timers thought so. It is interesting to note that this is the only statistically significant discrepancy found in the attitudes of part-timers as compared to full-timers; otherwise their perceptions on the distribution of influence within the board matched quite well. It is reasonable, therefore, to assume that insofar as the influence of government officials is concerned both full-timers and part-timers alike tended to exaggerate – in opposite directions – and the real degree of influence is somewhere in between that perceived by full-timers and that perceived by part timers.

Another thing worthwile noting is that both the minister responsible and the minister of finance are perceived to have more influence in Israel than in Britain. In fact, in Israel, their influence is perceived to almost match that of the board. Especially noticeable is the negligible amount of influence attributed to employees, consumers, and the "public at large." This finding supports the contentions of various writers (Robson 1962; Hanson 1962; Prakash 1963) that these bodies have little influence on state public enterprises.

As is obvious from the above discussion, part-timers are considered much less influential than full-timers. They themselves, as well as their full-time colleagues recognize that they lack the knowledge, expertise, experience, and involvement necessary for taking an equal share in policy formation. Yet, they are there. They exist. The question then arises to what extent is their existence justified in their own eyes and in the eyes of the their full-time partners. What functions are they perceived to fulfill? To what extent are these functions perceived as vital, or, conversely, as marginal?

One function most frequently mentioned by board members in Britain, part-timers and full-timers alike, was the capability of part-timers to take a "broader view," to "see things in a different way" than full-timers.

To cite some of the full-timers:

Outside directors are of great help; they see things in a different way than management, which is too immersed in daily affairs. They take a broader view (B 1–5).

They look at things in different ways . . .; they make us think about things which we would not have thought about otherwise. For example, they contribute much to the question of how to keep the business sound and safe in inflation (B 3–3).

They bring in experience of the world outside, which career people don't have (B 3–1).

Part-timers:

Part-time board members are a valuable assistance. They bring in expertise (according to their particular background). Full-timers tend to be insular in their outlook (B 5-4).

Yet, the different outlook of part-timers is also a source of tension between them and full-timers:

Part-timers are a peculiar group. They cannot know much about what happened in between board meetings. Some are very good indeed on giving general advice; this is the best way. But some want to be part of the management, and then they become dangerous.

It can be extremely irritating when you have dealt with a serious problem and probed it for a long time, and then some part-timers (who don't know much) say 'but we do it differently.'

In general, I would say that their function is the levelling of a view. But they are not of the family (Deputy Chairman, B 5–2).

The comments make it quite clear that in Britain part-timers are welcomed as advisers, people who can contribute from their experience to those holding executive responsibilities; there is, however, some ambivalence and reluctance to accept them as equals in the decision-making process.

In Israel, in contrast to Britain, part-timers and full-timers alike did not consider, generally, that part-timers contributed much in the way of special expertise and wider outlook. This would be expected in view of the high proportion of government officials on the Israeli boards.

On the other hand, in Israel as well as in Britain board members agreed that part-timers fulfilled, at times, important mediating functions, on behalf of the corporation, vis-à-vis government and other public bodies.

They have contacts with ministers and other influential people, and can put in a word for the corporation (B 3–4; full-timer).

There are two board members who function as a link with government. Mr. "X" who was a civil servant and is now retired; he knows the inner workings of government, the inner machinery, and is called often by management to attend and advise on various issues related to government. Mr. "Y" who has political contacts in the Welsh area, is used in relation to the Welsh scene (B 4–1; part-timer).

I expect Mr. "Z" [who is an official in one of the ministries, M. D.] to help me when I ask something from the ministry (I 17–377; full-timer).

In Israel, however, the mediating function of government officials was looked at by full-timers as a mixed blessing. In fact, it revealed itself as a source of severe strain between the two.

Mr. "X" sits in our board and has access to all the information. As a result, he knows in advance all our arguments and will have ready answers when we come with our case to his ministry (I 25–122).

There is a tremendous advantage in having "inside information." It is for this reason that I am against the representation of the ministries on the board (I 11–136).

Mr. "Y" doesn't see it as his duty to take care of our affairs. He sits on our board and has access to all the information which he then uses to counter our demands when they are brought before the Ministry of Finance. This is very unfair (I 17–337).

Part-timers, as full-timers in both Britain and Israel agreed, also fulfill important advisory functions in relation to publicly sensitive issues; they also serve as a source of information in this regard. Their opinion is sought, among others, because of their contacts with a variety of segments of the "public at large."

One of the major functions attributed to part-timers on the boards of public enterprise is the custody of the "public interest." The empirical question in an analysis of role perceptions becomes then: Do part-timers, indeed, regard themselves as the custodians of the public interest, and, if so, to what extent? Are they regarded as such by their full-time partners?

When confronted with the question whether they regard as one of their functions "take[ing] care of the public interest," all part-timers answered in the affirmative. Similarly when a general question about "the functions of part-timers on the board" was put before the board members, the majority tended to mention in one way or the other the custody of the public interest:

They [the part-timers, M. D.] are those who bring issues of public interest to the board. The board would never consider these issues otherwise (B 4–1).

It is important to have members who are not inbred; who can take care of the public interest (B 3–1).

However, when presented with the dilemma, whose interests should they represent "in case of a conflict of interests between the parties determining the corporation's fate and policy" the majority of part-timers in Britain (more than 70%) replied that they should represent the interests of the corporation!

In Israel, the picture is somewhat different. Only about 47% of the *total* sample of part-timers thought that they should represent the interests of the corporation. But, as can be seen from Table 7.6 there is a large and statistically significant difference between the attitudes of the officials representing the various ministries and the rest of the board members. Whereas the majority of the latter identifies with the corporation, only 35% of the former do so.

Table 7.6   Responses to: ". . . whose interests should you represent . . .?" (Israel) (percentages)

Membership Category	The Interests of:			
	The Corpo-ration	The Public	The Go-vernment	Total
Part-timers: officials	35.0	4.4	60.6	100.0
Part-timers: representatives of public	60.0	15.0	25.0	100.0
Full-timers	92.9	7.1	0.0	100.0

But what is more interesting, is that only a very small majority in both groups identifies with the interests of "the public at large." Let us look at some of the more typical statements which could throw some light on our findings.

This is a very difficult question. I believe that it is most relevant in relation to a conflict of interests between the corporation and the government, since "the public" is an amorphous thing. I have to represent the interests of the ministry (official representing the ministry responsible; I 17–107).

I have to represent the interests of the government. I have been appointed by the minister of development and by the recommendation of the minister of finance. I do not always agree with the minister of finance, but his considerations are important. I do not know what "the public" is. If my friends in the ministry of finance should argue that some action should be taken (or avoided) because of the public interest, I will listen very carefully to their arguments (representative of "the public"; I 20–263).

I see myself first and foremost as the representative of the corporation. . . .

Usually, the decisive interest is the interest of the corporation. Those who do not represent the various ministries, are, more or less, like myself. Those who represent the ministries tend very often to defend the position of the respective ministry (representative of "the public"; I 29–104).

I have to ask for the opinion of the minister responsible when no clear directive exists. If the directive given is against my best judgment, I still have to act according to it or otherwise resign. Usually, the interests of the corporation are important, but the directives of the government and the ministry must be carried out (representative of a ministry; I 18–282).

What is obvious, is that both, those holding an office in one of the ministries as well as those representing "the public," find it difficult to identify with what seems rather a vague and undefined concept, "the public interest." Rather, they tend to look for some tangible and more meaningful anchoring points.

One such anchoring point is apparently provided by the legal framework which sees in the director "a trustee of the corporation." This would explain the tendency of those board members in Israel who do not hold an office in one of the ministries, as well as the tendency of the majority of part-timers in Britain, to identify with the interests of the corporation.

The officials serving as directors in Israel, however, are faced with the dilemma of "double loyalty." The majority declared that they see themselves first of all as representing the interests of government. Many of them believed that in doing so they are in fact representing the public interest:

It is my duty to represent the interests of the ministry. In doing this I am in fact representing a wide array of interests (I 17–210).

However, a substantial proportion of officials serving as directors on the

various boards, observed that our question raises a difficult problem; that
they are faced with a real dilemma whenever the problem of conflicting
interests arises. Though they tended to give priority to the interests of
government, this is by no means an automatic reaction for many of them.
Often, they confessed, they tend to take decisions on an ad-hoc basis.
Being cross pressured, compromises, or even avoiding decisions al-
together, seem to provide a convenient way out:

I believe that it is my duty to represent the interests of the corporation. But this
leads to a kind of schizophrenia, the moment I leave the premises of the corporation. At that moment, I am again an official in the Ministry of Finance (I 17–356).

Usually, the interests of the corporation are important to me; but one has to
comply with directives of the government and of the ministry. Whenever there is a
conflict between my job as an official, and my job as a director, I am looking for a
compromise, or, I prefer that the decision is taken by somebody else, when I feel
that the conflict prevents me from reaching the right decision.
The decisions I make are in fact on an "ad-hoc" basis (I 18–282).

Summary. Though there is general agreement among board members
that the board should function mainly as a policy-making body, part-
timers and full-timers diverge in their views as to the nature of policy-
making powers which should be entrusted to the board.

Part-timers believe that the board should be vested with decision-making powers concerning major long-term policy issues and current policy
matters, which may have important implications for the national economy. On the other hand, the attitude of full-timers is that decision-making
is mainly a matter for the executive management. The board should function mainly as a body entrusted with powers to approve major long-term
policy decisions; current policy matters should be left entirely to the discretion of the executive management.

In practice, according to the great majority of board members, the
board functions mainly as a body *approving* decisions brought before it by
the executive management. On some occasions, the original proposals of
the executive management are modified as a result of board discussions.

Most board members attribute to the executive management more influence, in matters of policy-making, than they attribute to the board or
the government. Whereas the board, as a body, and the government are
considered to possess a moderate degree of influence on the objectives of
the corporation, most board members view the employees, the consumers, and the "public at large" as nearly completely uninfluential.

The lesser influence of the board, in comparison to that of the executive
management, obviously reflects the fact that it is partly composed of part-

time members. There is general agreement among full-timers and part-timers alike that part-timers lack the necessary knowledge, expertise, experience, and involvement to be able to take an equal share with full-timers in policy formation. In consequence, the policy-making functions of part-timers are greatly reduced. In Britain they function primarily as advisers, bringing in expertise in particular fields and "a broader outlook." They also function occasionally as a link between the corporation and other outside groups, government included.

In Israel, part-timers act mainly as a link between the corporation and government or various interest groups, depending on whether they are officials in the various ministries or whether they officially represent various interest groups. In Israel the advisory function of part-timers is of marginal importance in comparison to the function of linking the corporation with government and various other outside groups.

Whereas in Britain the mediating function of part-timers vis-à-vis outside groups is regarded by the executive management as a positive contribution to the corporation, in Israel, full-timers have a very ambivalent attitude toward it. This ambivalency is mainly due to the belief that the loyalty to the corporation of part-timers, and especially of the government officials among them and those representing various interest groups, is questionable. Our findings indicate that insofar as government officials are concerned this is indeed so in practice: the majority clearly stated that their loyalty is due first and foremost to the government.

Though the majority of part-timers declare that they see as one of their important duties to safeguard the public interest, the public interest does not occupy an important place in their actual role perceptions as board members. Only a very small minority thought that one of their main functions on the board is to look after the public interest, and very few thought that it is their duty to represent the public interest in case of a conflict of interests. In other words, the custody of the public interest is a widely accepted norm among part-time board members, with very little behavioral implications.

Chapter Eight
Role-Stress Among the Chief Executives

It was argued that an analysis of role-stress among the top-level active managers in public enterprise could reveal whether and to what extent certain situations perceived to have a negative psychological effect on the occupants of these positions, do indeed have the assumed effects. Specifically, the questions are: (1) Do top-level managers indeed exhibit feelings of anomie, normlessness, when faced with a conflicting goal structure and with conflicting demands as to the conduct of the enterprise? (2) Do they indeed experience role-stress when confronted with cross-pressures from various interest groups or when confronting a situation of conflict between the various interested parties? (3) Do they indeed feel powerless and show signs of apathy when faced with a situation in which the discretionary powers they actually possess do not match those they perceive as necessary for fulfilling their roles?

From among those in charge of the day-to-day management, we chose, for obvious reasons, to focus on the chief executive officers (CEOs): They, more than anyone else, are most likely to be exposed to the conflictful situations detailed above. Being placed in an interface position between the day-to-day management and the board they can hardly escape the cross-pressures emanating from these two bodies. Moreover, in most cases the chief executives are also members of the board and wearing these two "hats" can hardly give them a feeling of complacency and ease.

Ideally we would have liked to collect and examine the relevant data from both the British and Israeli samples. Yet, we had to confine ourselves to the Israeli sample. The reason was that the British sample contained too few cases to allow the required statistical analyses, and to combine the data from both samples did not seem appropriate in view of the significant differences between the two settings. Obviously, this choice which circumstances dictated has resulted in some loss of information. Yet, we believe that it has not impaired the investigation much since from among the two settings, the Israeli setting provided the far better ground for investigating the issues specified. The reason is that because of certain features of the Israeli context the types of conflicts mentioned were more likely to arise in that context than in the British context. First, there was relatively more room in the Israeli context for divergent interpretations of the objectives and modes of operation of the enterprises: The Ordinary Corporations Act under which the public enterprises in Israel were incorporated, unlike the British statutes, allowed for much flexibility in the definition of objectives and modes of operation of the enterprises, which in turn, opened the door for divergent and conflictual views on these subjects. Second, in Israel, in contrast to Britain, no regulations existed in regard to the board's structure and composition, its mode of operation, and its areas of authority. This left plenty of room for the formation of divergent interpretations as to the areas of authority and responsibility of the boards. Finally, the fact that the boards in Israel were composed partly of the representatives of various ministries and partly of the representatives of various interest groups legitimized, in a way, the expression of divergent interests and enhanced the chances of conflict on the board.

Indeed, the data from our research lend support to the above contentions. For example, the data in Chapter 5 show that in Israel as compared to Britain, board members tend relatively more to perceive the existence of multiple goals, and there is less agreement on what the most important goal is. The Israeli data also show a wider spectrum of divergent interests on the boards (see Chapter 7). Finally, as we have seen, the data indicate that in Israel there is wide disagreement about the decision-making functions of the boards.

The Measurement of Conflict

The framework of the investigation was broader than required by the basic questions posed above: The aim was to investigate how the variety of divergent orientations, expectations, and role perceptions that revealed themselves in the previous chapters, affect the CEOs in terms of felt role-stress. Specifically the investigation focused on the following *types* of conflictful situations:

1. One situation is that in which the views of the CEOs diverge from those of other board members (BMs). This type of conflict was identified by Kahn et al. (1964) as "person role conflict," a situation in which the "focal" person is in disagreement with his role-partners.

2. A second situation is that in which the BMs disagree among themselves. This type of conflict was identified by Kahn et al. (1964) as "in-

tersender role conflict," a situation in which the focal person is exposed to conflicting expectations from his role-partners.

3. Finally, a situation in which the discretionary powers possessed by the CEOs do not match those regarded by them as essential for adequately fulfilling their roles.

The disagreements specified in (1) and (2) were investigated in regard to the following areas and questions:

(a) The objectives of the corporation:
   1. "What are, in your opinion, the objectives of this corporation? Rank the objectives according to degree of importance."
(b) Criteria for resource allocation:
   2. "Would you approve of an investment if it is profitable to the corporation but not to the economy?"
   3. "Is the existence of the corporation justified without profitability?"
(c) The relationship between the corporation and government:
   4. "In your opinion, should this corporation be used for implementing the government's policy in the following areas: employment/wages/prices/investment?"
(d) The allocation of decision-making powers in relation to central issues of policy-making and resource allocation:
   5. "In whom should the authority to *decide* the following matters be vested ...?"
   6. "In whom should the authority to *approve* the following matters be vested ...?"
(e) Whose interests should be given priority:
   7. "In case of a conflict of interests between the parties determining the corporation's fate and its policies, whose interests is it your job to represent?"

The perceived discrepancies between the desired and actual allocation of decision-making powers (para. (3) above) were measured by means of questions (d-5) and (d-6) above and a rephrasing of these questions to read: "In whom *is* ..." instead of "In whom *should* ..."

The measures employed for measuring the *degree* of conflict in relation to each of the above questions are described in Appendix H. Basically they consist of indices that measure the degree of congruency between the views of the parties involved. In each case a formula was chosen that best fitted the issue investigated.

The Measurement of Role-Stress

For measuring role-stress among the CEOs a questionnaire, reproduced as Appendix C, was used. The questionnaire was based on the research of Kahn et al. (1964) and Rizzo and House (1970). The questionnaire consists of a leading question:

• "To what extent do you worry, in your job, about the following things . . ."

This was followed by ten items describing role-stress such as:

• "The lack of clear policies and guideliness to help me in my job."
• "I am not always clear about the scope of my authority."

In relation to each item, respondents were requested to choose from among the following response categories:

Never/Rarely/Often/Almost all the time/All the time,

the one that best reflects how they feel about the situation described by the item.

The responses to the above questionnaire were factor-analyzed and three principal factors were obtained which served for constructing three distinct indices of role-stress as follows (see Appendix I for a full description of the method for deriving the indices):

1. One type of role-stress was labelled *"Anomie"* (A) since it reflects a situation characterized by feelings of normlessness and powerlessness. The items composing the index were:
• "The lack of a clear policy and guiding rules which would help me in fulfilling my job."
• "The feeling that I do not have enough influence over the decisions and actions of my superiors, concerning the corporation and myself."
2. A second type of role-stress was labelled *"Intersender Role Stress"* (IRS), since it reflects a situation characterized by conflicting pressures from role-partners. The items composing the index were:
• "I work in a situation of conflicting demands and contradictory orders."
3. A third type of role-stress was labelled *"Self Role Stress"* (SRS) since it reflects a situation characterized by a feeling of being compelled to do things with which one does not fully agree. The items composing the index were:
• "Sometimes I must bypass an order or deviate from an accepted policy in order to carry out my duties."
• "I must sometimes do things in my job which are against my better judgment."

The scores for each index were calculated by adding up the scores on the items composing the index. From here onwards we shall refer to the three indices as "the indices of role-stress."

A series of correlational analyses between the above indices of role-stress and the indices of conflict previously discussed were used for examining whether and to what extent the conflictful situations specified are related to role stress among the CEOs.

The Relationship Between Disagreements Among the BMs and Disagreements Between the BMs and the CEOs and Role Stress Among the CEOs

The findings indicate that, generally, role-stress among the CEOs is moderate. For example, indications of extreme stress, i. e., replies of being worried "all the time" or "most of the time" about the ten situations described, were found in relation to about only half of the situations. The highest average score was found in relation to item 2 (see Appendix H): "I have to carry out my job under substantial and often contradictory pressures." The lowest average score was found in relation to items 5 and 9: "I am not always clear about the scope of my authority," and, "It is not clear what the scope and the areas of responsibility of my job are." The average scores relating to the items composing the final indices are displayed in Table 8.1.

Some of the CEOs exhibited more role-stress than others. For example, the highest average score found among the CEOs was 4.20, while the lowest was 1.00.

The relatively moderate amount of role-stress found among the CEOs should come as no surprise: The pertinent literature indicates that individuals in managerial positions and especially those at the top of the ladder, are, on average, relatively more "immune" to role-stress than others, and that such relative immunity is perhaps an important trait in the process of selection and self-selection to such positions. The CEOs in public enterprise should be no exception to this. If at all we would expect them to be even more "tough-skinned" than their colleagues in private enterprise, who are not faced with the fundamental dilemmas existing in public enterprise.

But in this research the central question is not the absolute amount of

Table 8.1   Average scores for items composing the indices of role-stress

Anomie
- "The lack of a clear policy and guiding rules which would help me in fulfilling my job."
  ($\overline{X}$ = 2.85; S. D. = 1.23)

- "The feeling that I do not have enough influence over the decisions and actions of my superiors concerning the corporation and myself."
  ($\overline{X}$ = 2.64; S. D. = 1.15)

Self-Role-Stress
- "Sometimes I must bypass an order or deviate from an accepted policy in order to carry out my duties."
  ($\overline{X}$ = 2.35; S. D. = 1.01)

- "I must do sometimes things in my job that are against by better judgment"
  ($\overline{X}$ = 2.36; S. D. = 1.28)

Intersender-Role-Stress
- "I work in a situation of conflicting demands and contradictory orders."
  ($\overline{X}$ = 2.36; S. D. = 1.08)

role-stress among the CEOs in public enterprise. Rather, as already emphasized, the question is whether disagreements, typical to public enterprise, between the CEO and his colleagues on the board and between the board members themselves are an important source of role-stress among those carrying the daily burden of managing the public enterprise. We turn now to the findings relating to this question.

Tables 8.2 and 8.3 present the results of the analyses relating to disagreements between the CEOs and BMs (CEOs : BMs) and those relating to disagreements among the BMs themselves (BMs : BMs).

There are two major ways of looking at the findings. One is to examine them in a more general way in an attempt to discover general trends. The other is to look at the details in order to gain some insight into the specific relationships between prevalent disagreements on the boards and role stress among the CEOs.

There are three important angles for examining the general trends. One such angle is to inquire which of the two types of conflictful situations, disagreements between CEOs : BMS or disagreements among the BMs : BMs, cause more role-stress among the CEOs in the areas investigated. Such inquiry could indicate the *types of conflicts* that have a greater impact on the CEOs.

Table 8.2 Disagreements between chief executives and board members and role-stress among chief executives (correlation coefficients)

Index of role-stress	Type of disagreement		Resource allocation criteria				Allocation of decision-making powers. Authority	
				Existence of Relationship				
	Objectives	Investments	Corporation	Government	Interests		to decide	to approve
Anomie (A)	-0.17	0.21	0.34 (0.06)	0.32 (0.10)	0.52 (0.01)		0.15	0.09
Self role-stress (SRS)	-0.06	-0.11	0.22	-0.07	0.26		-0.03	0.22
Intersender role-stress (IRS)	-0.33 (0.05)	-0.47 (0.02)	0.13	0.00	0.27 (0.10)		-0.08	0.29 (0.09)

n: CEOs = 17; BMs = 42; total = 59. The numbers in parantheses show levels of significance for $P \leq 0.10$

Table 8.3 Disagreements among board members themselves and role-stress among chief executives (correlation coefficients)

Index of role-stress	Type of disagreement	Resource allocation criteria				Allocation of decision-making powers	
		Existence of Relationship				Authority	
	Objectives	Investments	Corporation	Government	Interests	to decide	to approve
Anomie (A)	0.41 (0.06)	-0.04	0.10	0.35 (0.08)	0.22	0.49 (0.02)	0.22
Self role-stress (SRS)	-0.33 (0.10)	0.18	0.20	0.17	-0.34 (0.07)	0.08	-0.23
Intersender role-stress (IRS)	-0.16	0.11	0.27	0.00	0.17	0.04	-0.46 (0.02)

n: CEOs = 17; BMs = 42; total = 59. The numbers in parentheses show levels of significance for $P \leq 0.10$

A second angle is to examine the *areas* in which conflicts between the CEOs : BMs and conflicts among BMs : BMs are related to role stress among the CEOs. This could give us an indication about which areas are more "sensitive," in the sense of being likely to produce role-stress among chief executives in conflictful situations. Finally, a third angle is to inquire which type of role-stress is more prevalent among the CEOs: is it anomie, self-role-stress, or intersender role-stress? This could serve as an indication to the *nature of stress* more likely to arise as a result of the conflictual situations investigated.

The first question requires a review of the significant positive correlations in both tables presented above. Such a review shows that there are more such correlations in Table 8.2, referring to conflicts between the CEOs and BMs, than in Table 8.3, referring to conflicts among the BMs themselves. This suggests that on the whole, in relation to the issues investigated, there are more sources of role-stress from disagreements between the CEOs and the BMs than from disagreements among the BMs themselves.

The second question requires an examination of the significant positive correlations in the various areas in both tables. Such an examination reveals that there is only one area, the approval of investments that are not profitable, where the existence of conflicting views is not associated with some type of role-stress among the CEOs. Second it shows that in three areas, the nature of *relationships between the corporation and government*, the *type of interests to be given priority* in case of a conflict of interests, and the *desired allocation of decision-making powers*, there are more significant positive correlations than in the other areas. These latter findings suggest that disagreements in the above areas create more role-stress among the CEOs than disagreements in the other areas investigated.

Finally, the third question requires an overview of the significant positive correlations associated with each type of role conflict. Such an overview indicates that there are more positive correlations in regard to "anomie" than in regard to the other types of role-stress. Moreover, self-role-stress (SRS) is negatively associated with certain types of conflicts, but is not related positively to any type of conflict, which rules it out as a source of role-stress among the CEOs in relation to the issues investigated. We also note that while anomie (A) is positively associated with both types of disagreements, CEOs : BMs and BMs : BMs, intersender role-stress (IRS) is positively associated with disagreements between CEOs : BMs only.

An examination of the specific relationships reveals an interesting and rather complex picture; much more complex than the one to be expected on the basis of the assumptions prompting this investigation. Thus, a review of the significant relationships in Table 8.3, row one, shows that the CEOs react, as expected, with feelings of anomie (A) – normlessness and powerlessness – when they are confronted by a board divided on such basic issues as the objectives of the enterprise, its relationship with government, and the allocation of decision-making powers. But, in addition, the findings in Table 8.2 also show that the CEOs react in a similar way, i. e., with feelings of anomie (A) also when they *themselves* disagree with other BMs on certain issues such as whether the existence of the enterprise is justified without profitability, the nature of relationships with government, and the interests that should be given priority in case of a conflict of interests on the board.

What explains these latter findings? Why do CEOs react with feelings of anomie – normlessness and powerlessness – when they disagree with their role-partners? Why do they simply not accept the directives of the board and carry them out, as one would suppose they *should* do? One explanation suggesting itself is that CEOs regard themselves as fully entitled to have their *independent* views about the conduct of the enterprise rather than viewing themselves as the mere executors of the directives of others: As a result, when they are opposed by the board and are not able to act according to their best judgment, they tend to withdraw from their roles rather than to act in obedience to the views imposed upon them.

A review of the significant relationships in Table 8.2, row three, also shows that in regard to two areas, the authority to approve major policies and resource allocation decisions, and giving priority to certain interests in case of a conflict of interests on the board, a disagreement between the CEOs : BMs is associated with intersender role-stress (IRS) among the CEOs. This finding is somewhat unexpected and requires an explanation: Why do CEOs react with a feeling of being exposed to "conflicting demands and contradictory orders" where there is disagreement between them and other BMs? One explanation suggesting itself is that, according to previous research in Israel, the board is often bypassed and CEOs deal directly with the responsible minister (Aharoni 1970: 62–65). Under such circumstances it is possible that CEOs experience intersender role-stress when the views of some other board members conflict with the directives given to them directly by the minister and bypassing the board.

The absence of significant positive correlations between the IRS index and disagreements among BMs : BMs, contrary to what we would have expected, poses another question: Why do CEOs *not* experience intersender role-stress when the BMs disagree among themselves on various matters? Seemingly, the explanation suggested above applies also in this case: If the board can be bypassed, the CEOs do not need to feel cross-pressured by the different views of the BMs; however, they do feel *disoriented* by such disagreements as our findings discussed above show. More than that, some findings indicate that disagreements among the BMs themselves might *lessen* the degree of role-stress among the CEOs. Thus, as Table 8.3 shows, disagreements among the BMs : BMs on the allocation of decision-making powers are negatively correlated with intersender role-stress (IRS) among the CEOs.

A significant negative correlation was also found between disagreements among the BMs on the objectives of the enterprise and on the interests to be given priority in case of a conflict of interests on the board – and self-role-stress (SRS) among CEOs. Merton's proposition (1957) stating that a position-incumbent, who is subject to conflicting demands from his role-partners, "often becomes cast in the role of *tertius gaudens,* the third party who draws advantage from the conflict of others," may explain these findings: When BMs have conflicting interests and divergent goal orientations, CEOs would be able to exploit this situation in order to further their interests and pursue their own will. This would obviously result in less self-role-stress among the CEOs. Similarly, CEOs would experience less self-role-stress when BMs disagree on how decision-making powers should be allocated since this situation would, in all probability, enhance the freedom of CEOs to act as they deem fit.

The Relationship Between a Discrepancy in the Perceived Actual and Desired Powers of the Board and Role-Stress Among the CEOs

A major question posed relates to the prevalent assumption that the active management in public enterprise might react negatively when it perceives itself as having too little autonomy. One way to investigate this assumption empirically is to examine whether, as expected, CEOs do indeed react with feelings of role-stress when faced with a situation in which a discrepancy exists between the discretionary powers they perceive as essential for fulfilling their roles and those they actually possess. Only two of the role-stress indices, anomie (A) and self-role-stress (SRS), were suitable for this investigation; intersender role-stress (IRS), referring to role-stress stemming from cross-pressures of one's role partners, was obviously not relevant for this investigation. The association between the indices of role-stress and the indices of incongruency was measured by using Kendall's correlation coefficient. The results of the analysis are presented in Table 8.4.

Table 8.4 Role-stress among chief executives and discrepancies in actual and desired allocation of decision-making powers (correlation coefficients)

	Discrepancies in:	
	Authority to decide	Authority to approve
Anomie	0.50 (0.01)	0.54 (0.004)
Self role-stress	0.03	0.27 (0.09)

The numbers in parentheses show levels of significance

In general, the findings indicate that there is indeed a positive relationship between role-stress among CEOs and an incongruency between the perceived actual and the desired allocation of decision-making powers. This is especially true in relation to the index of anomie: as can be seen, significant positive correlations have been found between this index and both indexes of incongruency, that concerning the authority to decide and that concerning the authority to approve of various policies and resource allocation issues.

The above findings indicate that, as might have been expected, CEOs do indeed react with feelings of anomie – normlessness and powerlessness – to a situation where they are not in full possession of those discretionary powers they regard as essential for an adequate role fulfillment. Moreover, CEOs seem also, according to our findings, to react not only with feelings of anomie but also with feelings labelled as self-role-stress when the actual allocation of authority to approve of certain policies and resource allocation decisions does not match the desired allocation of authority.

Summary. Our findings indicate that disagreements on the board of directors about various basic issues such as the objectives of the corporation, the criteria for resource allocation, the interests to be given priority in the case of a conflict of interests, the nature of relationships between the enterprise and the government, and the allocation of decision-making powers, are indeed, as expected, a source of role stress among the CEOs. So is an incongruency between the perceived actual and desired allocation of decision-making powers. Indeed, the findings show that very few of the conflictful situations examined, have no impact, in terms of role-stress, on the CEOs. Yet, a closer look reveals that certain types of disagreements are more likely to be associated with role-stress among the CEOs than others. Thus, we found that in the areas investigated, disagreements between the CEOs: BMs are more likely to result in some forms of role-stress among the CEOs than disagreements among the BMs: BMs themselves. Similarly, disagreements related to certain areas are more likely to be associated with some form of role-stress among the CEOs than disagreements related to other areas. Thus, in relation to three areas: the nature of relationships between the corporation and government, the type of interests to be given priority in case of a conflict of interests, and the desired allocation of decision-making powers, disagreements are relatively more related to role-stress among the CEOs than in other areas. A possible explanation is that role-stress is more likely to occur when the disagreements relate to issues that concern the daily conduct of the corporation than when they relate to basic values such as what justifies the raison d'être of the corporation, or what criteria should be used in deciding on major investments.

One type of role-stress, anomie, seems to be more prevalent than the other two types. Moreover, self-role-stress was not found to be associated with any of the BMs: BMs and CEOs: BMs disagreements investigated. This type of role-stress was, however, found, as expected, to be positively related to the existence of an incongruency between the actual and desired allocation of the authority to approve of various policy and resource-allocation issues. Both types of incongruency, that between the actual and desired authority to decide, as well as that between the actual and desired authority to approve of various policy and resource-allocation issues, were also found to be positively associated with feelings of anomie.

The findings indicate that in certain cases a conflictful situation may have an opposite effect to that expected. Thus, disagreements among BMs: BMs about the objectives of the corporation and about the interests to be given priority in case of a conflict of interests have been found to be *negatively* associated with self-role-stress among the CEOs. Similarly, disagreements between BMs: BMs on the allocation of the authority to approve of various policy and resource allocation issues, have been found to be negatively associated with intersender role-stress among the CEOs. The suggested explanation given for these findings is that when board members disagree among themselves CEOs may feel freer to act according to their own convictions.

Chapter Nine
Implications of the Research Findings

It was argued in Chapter 2 that certain organizational problems concerning the board of directors in public enterprise could be more adequately dealt with and the debates surrounding them could be greatly reduced if more empirical knowledge could be made available about the orientations, attitudes, and role perceptions of those actually engaged in the conduct of public enterprises. It is possible now to relate the findings presented in the preceding chapters to these problems and to examine their organizational implications. Whenever feasible, an attempt will be made to broaden the perspective by bringing our findings into the orbit of relevant organizational theories which could assist in their interpretation and which could provide a basis for their evaluation.

One major problem delineated in Chapter 2 concerns the function of the board in public enterprise. One major division of opinion rests on whether the board should be entrusted with major policy-making functions or not. A secondary division of opinion is between those who believe that the board could be made responsible for commercial efficiency but not for the implementation of other objectives of public interest, and those who believe that it is not necessary to restrain its responsibilities to commercial matters. The division, it was argued, is in essence between those who perceive identification with, and orientations toward the official goals of the corporation as largely unproblematic, and those who view them as problematic. The latters' concern is mainly over two things. First, that the leadership of the corporation, driven by self-interest, will prefer pursuit of their own selfish goals over pursuit of the corporation's official objectives. Second, that the leadership, even if not predisposed to subvert the official objectives to self-interest, would find it difficult to identify with, and orient itself toward the public interest. In this latter respect, emphasis is put on the intangibility of the public interest and on the difficulty of translating it into consistent and tangible guiding principles for policy-making and managerial purposes.

It should not come as a surprise that these divisions of opinion concerning managerial motivation among students of public enterprise reflect, in fact, certain broader divisions existing among organizational scientists. Thus, Simon, an eminent organizational scientist, maintains that individuals tend to internalize those organizational values which define their roles (Simon 1964; 1976: 198 ff), which implies that one can reasonably expect the leadership of an organization to identify with its official goals and orient itself toward these goals. However, other organizational scientists, whose views have no less support, emphasize the pursuit of various personal interests as the major motivating factor (Cyert and March 1963; Georgiou 1973).

An in-between position is taken by those viewing the social and professional background of organizational leaders and their personal inclinations as a major determinant of their goal orientations (Perrow 1961; Guth and Tagiuri 1965). For example, Escobar (1982) adopts this view in analysing the orientations of public-enterprise managers. He distinguishes between *commissars,* often from a civil service background, which give high priority to wishes of government representatives, and *engineers,* often from a business background, who are profit and growth oriented. Aharoni (1986: 291–294) joins in and adds to these two types "the military type, [and] three more types ... public entrepreneurs, empire builders and leaders." Public entrepreneurs, "are not motivated by pecuniary gain. They are instead driven by power, glory, prestige and the high need for achievement...." "Empire builders derive satisfaction from serving the public rather than private interest and are mainly motivated by the desire to build industrial and other empires of modern capital-intensive enterprise." Finally, there are the leaders "whose personal magnetism is the basis of their authority and power." Further Aharoni refers to the career path perceptions of the above leader types in order to explore their orientations: Commissars and military types perceive their career in government or in the armed forces. "They, therefore, protect themselves and are often conditioned to not making decisions – certainly not without prior clearance and authorization." "Engineers and leaders see their promotion opportunities mainly in economic enterprise...." "They ... perceive themselves as being constantly evaluated within a national market for managers...." "The empire builders are motivated mainly by the desire to build empires. Knowing that this is possible for them only in the public sector, they attempt to establish and nurture political power."

In a recent attempt to consolidate the various major views, Mohr (1973) avoids the question of prediction by postulating that the actual goal orientations of organizational leaders are empirical matters (Mohr 1973: 476–477).

Our findings indicate that such a view may not be justified. Nor do the personal- and professional-background and individual-inclinations approaches seem to do full justice to the subject. While the importance of such factors is surely not deniable, our research suggests that some broader lines may be drawn, anchored in certain role-related and systemic-placement contingencies. First, the results show that there is a substantial measure of consistency across individual organizations and across national settings in the orientations of the top-level leadership in public enterprise which implies that some generalizations may be justified. Second, however, the findings also indicate the existence of significant differences in orientations among various identifiable subgroups of the leadership. This suggests that all-too-sweeping generalizations concerning managerial motivation may not be warranted and calls for a more refined approach which would allow for the development of specific hypotheses concerning the formation of the varying goal orientations.

Most salient are the divergent orientations of full-time board members as opposed to those of part-time board members. The cleavages show most clearly in regard to the official goals of the enterprise – commercial efficiency and the public interest. While part-timers tend to de-emphasize profitability and emphasize instead various sociopolitical objectives, full-timers give clear preference to profitability over sociopolitical objectives. Moreover, full-timers exhibit an overwhelming concern with the well-being of the corporation, even more than with profitability – while part-timers seem largely unaffected by such considerations.

What seems most intriguing about these cleavages is that one can find support for each of the various theses presented in the debate about managerial motivation in the public enterprise, depending on which particular group one is focusing. Thus, the substantial concern found among full-timers for the well-being of the corporation seems to justify the self-interests thesis. The thesis that the public interest will be neglected in favor of commercial efficiency finds support in the data relating to the full-timers. This thesis, however, does not seem justified at all when the orientations of part-timers are considered.

It seems therefore reasonable to assume that the various theses may be justifiable only within the boundaries set by certain specifiable conditions. Thus, our findings indicate that even if self-interest is an important motivating force, it would not have a uniform impact on the goal orientations of the top-level leadership in public enterprise.

We suggest that the intensity or organizational involvement acts as an intervening variable to determine the extent to which self-interest becomes a major determinant in managerial goal orientations. The more intensive one's organizational involvement, the more would one's interests be tied to the well-being of the corporation, and the stronger, therefore, the incentive to formulate organizational objectives in terms which coincide with one's self-interest. The organizational involvement of full-timers is obviously very high – their status, prestige, and destiny are closely related to that of the corporation – which would explain their strong concern with its well-being. Conversely, the low organizational involvement of part-timers, whose major occupational interests lie outside the corporation, would explain their lesser concern with the well-being of the corporation, which is of little consequence to them personally.

Certain role-related differences seem to account for the differential orientations of full-timers as opposed to part-timers toward commercial efficiency, on the one hand, and the public interest, on the other. The predominant commercial orientation of full-timers seems to be related partly to their executive responsibilities. By virtue of these responsibilities, full-timers are faced with certain internal organizational problems which are of little concern to part-timers. The major such problems are the allocation of responsibilities and of material resources throughout the corporation, internal coordination involving what Barnard (1938) called "problems of efficiency," and the evaluation of performance.

According to Simon (1976), one effect of functional role differentiation is to focus the attention of role incumbents on the values which are of immediate concern to their roles, to the exclusion of other values (1976: 210 et passim).[1] According to this thesis executives can be expected to turn their attention to those organizational values which will allow them to cope satisfactorily with their internal organizational functions. As Warner and Havens (1968) note, this involves a shift from intangible goals toward more tangible system-maintenance goals.

The predominantly commercial orientation of full-timers can thus be partly explained in light of their role exigencies calling for *consistent* and *tangible* criteria, which a public-interest orientation could hardly provide. Support for this interpretation can be found in the fact that among the reasons given by the full-timers themselves for preferring the criterion of profitability, are its advantages as a guide for managerial action and decision-making and as a measure for managerial performance and efficiency.

Further support can be found in Aharoni and Lachman's paper (1982) "Can the manager's mind be nationalized?" In this paper, the authors report the research findings of a study in which the goal perceptions of chief executives in the private and public sectors are compared. The comparison shows that no significant differences exist between the two groups in their perceptions of the *actual* and *desired* influence of a series of environmental factors on their decisions: "Even 'public' environmental organs, such as ministries, trade unions, or public opinion, were not perceived to have more influence on public sector executives than on their private sector colleagues" (1982: 43). The authors conclude on the basis of their findings that "management is a general process irrespective of the type of organization or its goals" (1982: 45).

Since part-timers are not involved very much in internal organizational problems and since their self-interest is not closely interwoven with the status and well-being of the corporation one would expect to find among them a more balanced orientation toward the official goals of the public corporation. Yet, our findings indicate that there is a tendency among part-timers to orient themselves more toward various social objectives, whereas commercial efficiency is perceived by them more as a constraint than as an objective.

A proposition made by Parsons (1960) suggests a possible explanation for this finding. According to this proposition, functional role differentiation occurs at the upper managerial level of the organization, due to the fact that those bearing executive responsibilities cannot successfully fulfill at the same time the function of legitimation and community support for the organization. This latter function falls on the shoulders of those board members who are not part of the active management (1960: 68).

Consequently, nonexecutive board members may be expected to be particularly sensitive toward those aspects of corporate activity which affect its legitimation and public support, i. e., toward the public interest. Support for this interpretation may be found in the fact that part-timers do indeed perceive themselves as the custodians of the public interest, a self-role image which is not shared by full-timers.

Further support concerning the effect of functional responsibilities on the goal orientations of board members may be drawn from the fact that board chairmen were found to have an orientation intermediate to that of part-timers and full-timers. This conforms to the Lawrence and Lorsch (1967) thesis according to which the orientations of members fulfilling integrative functions in organizations are intermediate to those found among the subgroups they coordinate. Indeed, in view of the widely divergent orientation of part-timers and full-timers, the intermediate orientation of board chairmen seems essential for bridging the two groups and for achieving a measure of consensus on corporate policy and objectives.

In light of the foregoing analysis, the debate about the functions of the board of directors in public enterprise, at least insofar as it revolves around the question of managerial motivation, seems somewhat misplaced, mainly because it is conducted to a large extent in abstraction of those organizational and role-related factors which seem to be of cardinal importance in shaping the goal orientations of board members in public enterprise.

According to our analysis, the goal orientations of board members depend to a large degree on their organizational involvement and on the extent to which they fulfill executive responsibilities or not. Thus, a board dominated by, or composed mainly of executive members appointed for life could hardly be expected to be very much concerned with the public interest. Such a board would, in all probability, be concerned mainly with the continued existence of the corporation, with its growth, and with its commercial success. Conversely, a board composed mainly of part-timers – devoid of executive responsibilities and being appointed for a stipulated time – could be expected to orient itself mainly toward what its members would perceive as the public interest;[2] commercial efficiency would play a secondary role and would appear largely as a *constraint* in policy decisions rather than as an objective in itself.

The major implication is that the orientations of board members should not be regarded as given, as an unchangeable factor, in discussions concerning the functions of the board in public enterprise, but rather as a variable defined by certain specifiable parameters.

This variable and the parameters defining it could then be considered alongside other variables in dealing with the functions of the board in public enterprise.

A second question to which our investigation addressed itself concerns the problem of managerial autonomy. Our analysis in Chapter 2 shows that though there is widespread agreement among students of public enterprise that a substantial measure of managerial autonomy is a prerequisite for managerial motivation and initiative, there is no unanimity of opinion in regard to the actual organizational solutions to this problem. Some contend that the only solution lies in declaring commercial efficiency as the major guiding principle for the actions of the board. Others maintain that ministerial control could be instituted in regard to certain spheres of action or could be exercised through special formal directives, while still leaving substantial discretion to the management.

Yet a third opinion is that the problem might find its solution not so much in formal legislation but mainly through the development of mutual understanding between the board and government.

These proposed solutions can now be assessed in light of our findings. We may perhaps start by noting that the intensive preoccupation of those concerned with the organization and conduct of the public corporation with the question of managerial autonomy seems fully justified in light of the finding that there is indeed much concern among the board members themselves over this question. This is especially true in relation to full-timers whose striving for profitability is partly explained by their belief that profit is an essential prop of managerial autonomy, or conversely, that losses invite governmental intervention in the affairs of the corporation. This latter finding of ours fully coincides with the observation of other researchers of the public enterprise. Thus, Aharoni (1981), in his analysis of managerial discretion in public enterprise proposes that financial independence is a major factor contributing to such discretion.

The major concern of board members is, however, not over *absolute* autonomy; rather, what is actually desired is a measure of *functional* autonomy. Thus, board members generally agree that government should play a major role in long-term corporate planning. There is also general agreement that major investments should be subject to governmental approval.

But there is *general* objection among full-timers as well as part-timers to ad-hoc governmental interference, whether in order to implement certain short-term socioeconomic policies or for other reasons. One major reason given by board members for this objection is that such interference causes severe distortions in the implementation of long-term corporate plans. Other major reasons are that ad-hoc intervention impairs the ability of the corporation to react expediently to market forces, and that it exerts a negative impact on economic efficiency. The general frustrations expressed over the frequent ad-hoc governmental interventions in the affairs of the corporation seems thus related to a feeling among board members that such interventions interfere with the fulfillment of certain major managerial functions: mainly long-term corporate planning, the formulation of short- and long-term corporate strategy, and the achievement of economic efficiency.

Something about the forcefulness of these frustrations could be inferred by considering the fact that economic efficiency and the successful coping with environmental uncertainty are major managerial objectives. Governmental interference not only impairs the ability of the board to achieve these objectives, by intervening with the functions that are central for their achievement, but also introduces an additional element of uncertainty stemming from ad-hoc demands on corporate policy.

Regarding governmental authority insofar as it specifies the *long-range* terms of reference and the general rules of conduct within which the management is to operate, not only is there readiness to accept such authority but there is actually a desire among full-timers for such specifications. This desire is accompanied by the expectation that within the boundaries set by such rules board members should be free to act more or less at their discretion, without further outside intervention. This fits well with the theory advanced by organizational scientists according to which the function of rules and regulations is to delineate certain autonomous spheres within which those whose actions are delimited by these rules have freedom of action and are protected from arbitrary intervention by those who set the rules (Crozier 1964: 206–207; Gouldner 1954).

This also explains perhaps the reluctance of board members to leave the shelter of the general terms of reference regulating the corporation's relationships with government and engage in actions which necessitate ad-hoc cooperation with government, out of fear that this would lead to a loss of autonomy by opening a door to governmental intervention. A concrete example is the negative attitude of full-timers against involving the corporation in subsidized activities, justified by the argument that such involvement might lead to governmental intervention in the affairs of the corporation.

This argument is echoed so well by another research study on public enterprise that one cannot avoid citing it:

The less they depend on support out of the public purse – the idea of being subsidized out of the taxpayer's money is a distasteful one – the more independent and powerful they become. The feudal barons were strong as long as they were sustained by their local wealth and not dependent on favors bestowed upon them by the king (Frankel 1966: 167).

Turning now to examine the degree of autonomy actually experienced by board members, we find that notwithstanding the expressions of frustration concerning governmental intervention, they still feel that, in practice, government plays a much less important role, as compared to the board and to the active management, in determining the objectives of the corporation. This applies equally to Britain as well as to Israel. Indeed, in relation to Britain a recent independent study by Hickson et al. (1986) fully confirms our findings. In this study of 150 top-level decisions in a varied sample of businesses, Hickson et al. found that in *all* organizations, state-owned and private, "the main heavyweights are *internal*." But even more than that, "it is unexpected, and may be surprising, to find that the amount of governmental influence reported in the decision-making of the state-owned business organizations is not greater than in those that were private" (1986: 69).

In Israel too, as said, the balance of influence is clearly tipped internally. Yet, in comparison to Britain, the government is perceived to have a relatively greater share in determining the objectives of the corporation. A possible explanation is that the activities of public enterprises in Israel are not regulated by statutes. Consequently, in the absence of a body of rules which could protect the corporation from governmental intervention, such intervention in the affairs of the corporation is easier to exercise.

Notwithstanding the feeling of powerfulness vis-à-vis government, corporate autonomy is not taken for granted by the management. Rather, it is perceived as something which must be constantly and actively defended. One major and not rarely employed tactic is, so to speak, to confront the government with *faits accomplis*. Gouldner (1959) maintains that such behavior is greatly facilitated by functional autonomy, which isolates to some extent the organization from those wielding external authority over it. Indeed, our finding indicating that certain underlying elements of functional autonomy play an important role in the perceptions of the board members concerning their relatively powerful position strongly supports this thesis. Thus, as we have seen, board members perceive the need of coping with a competitive environment as a constraining force on the government's attempts to curb corporate autonomy. The implication is that the relative autonomy granted to the public corporation for functional purposes serves as an important means in the hands of the corporate management for the maintenance of managerial autonomy and, eventually, its expansion beyond legitimate boundaries. Indeed, this observation is shared by other researchers (Vernon 1981; Aharoni 1981; 1986).

Several things emerge from the above analysis. Perhaps the most salient thing is that the leadership in public enterprise exhibits, not surprisingly perhaps, a very strong drive for functional autonomy and is highly predisposed to take action and employ a variety of means in order to achieve it. The implication is that organizational arrangements aiming at the solution of the problem of managerial autonomy cannot be devised without considering the perceptions of those actually engaged in the conduct of the public enterprise as to the specific contents of such autonomy. Disregard of these conceptions can be dysfunctional not only in terms of managerial morale and initiative, but can also result in continuous conflicts with governmental authorities and in recurrent attempts to circumvent and resist governmental decisions concerning the policy of the corporation.

Second, it is quite clear that there is widespread readiness among board members and chief executives to accept governmental authority in long-term policy matters. This tends to disprove the contention that only organizational arrangements which would provide for full managerial autonomy (for example, conducting the corporation according to purely commercial principles) could be adequate.

Rather, and this is the third point, it seems that what those responsible for the public enterprise want is to have clear and relatively *stable* terms of reference within the boundaries of which they can expect to have full freedom of action. This sets certain conditions for the division of authority between the government and corporate management and implies that merely a clear division of authority – as suggested by some students of public enterprise (e.g., Maniatis 1968) – is not sufficient for the solution of the problem of managerial autonomy. Only by fulfilling the above conditions could such division be successful in terms of avoiding conflict between the leadership of the corporation and government.

A third key problem delineated in Chapter 2 concerns the composition of the board of directors. As indicated, there is no unanimity of opinion concerning two interrelated issues, the bases of recruitment and the terms of appointment to the board. The pivotal questions of debate are whether the board should be composed of impartial members or of representatives of interest groups, and whether full-time appointments are preferable to part-time appointments.

The major concern is over the implications of the bases of membership and the terms of appointment on the ability of the board to pay due attention to the public interest as well as commercial efficiency.

Thus, it is argued, that compared to factional representation, impartial representation is better suited to represent the interests of the public at large and to achieve the unity of opinion necessary for the formulation of consistent long-term corporate policies. A counter-argument is that impartial board members will have difficulties in determining the public interest and translating it into tangible corporate objectives.

Those in favor of long-term, full-time appointments argue that such appointments lead to the development of the expertise needed for the efficient conduct of the corporation. On the other hand, it is argued that long-term, full-time service in the corporation leads to an excessive identification with it and to a narrowing of horizons which would lead to the neglect of objectives which are in the public interest. Some students maintain that a mixed board composed partly of full-timers and partly of part-timers would provide a satisfactory solution to these dilemmas. Evidently, the whole debate derives its central meaning from the assumption that the policies of the corporation are and should be determined first and foremost by the board.

In light of this assumption it is interesting to note that according to our findings there is no unanimity of opinion in regard to the board's role in the policy-making process and that significant differences exist in this respect between full-timers and part-timers.

Partly, these differences of opinion stem from the varying goal orientations of full-timers and part-timers. Thus, full-timers, being concerned mainly with the commercial efficiency of the corporation, would like to have maximum decision flexibility in most matters and especially in those in which such flexibility is a prerequisite for commercial efficiency. They believe that the executive management should have full decision autonomy in current policy matters; they also tend to believe that the main role of the board in other matters should be that of approving proposals brought before it by the executive management. On the other hand, part-timers, who are more oriented toward various social objectives, are of the opinion that no issues should be exempt from approval by the board and, furthermore, that investment, pricing, and employment policies should be *actually decided* by the board and not merely approved by it.

The differences in outlook are probably also related to the quest, by those charged with executive responsibilities, for functional autonomy in relation to those matters for which they perceive themselves to be responsible. These would include first and foremost commercial and organizational efficiency, since it may be assumed that executives regard themselves best qualified to bear full responsibility for these matters because of their experience and close knowledge of the corporation's affairs. Their aspiration for autonomy in current policy matters may thus be seen as an attempt to achieve functional autonomy in those matters which have the most immediate impact on the efficiency and the commercial success of the corporation.

The major implication is that the mode of appointment to the board determines to a large extent the expectations board members have regarding its functioning. It may be expected that where the existing normative framework does not coincide with the role conceptions of the board members, pressures will develop to bring the functioning of the board closer to these conceptions. It may be further expected that conflicts would develop in mixed boards around questions relating to the division of authority between the board and the executive management. In light of this, it is questionable whether there is justification for the approach taken so far by some students of public enterprise according to which the mode of appointment to the board is considered independently from its policy-making functions.

Our findings regarding the actual role of the board in the policy-making process raise another question. According to these findings the board acts in practice mainly as a body before which policies proposed by the executive management are brought for approval; initiative rarely comes from the board. This implies that board members not fulfilling executive functions, especially part-timers, do not have an equal share to that of their full-time colleagues, in the decision-making process. Particularly they take only little part in the stage of alternative generation,[3] and their contribution is limited more or less to a later stage, when alternatives are weighed against one another and an actual course of action is chosen from among them.

This raises the question of whether the contributions supposed to be forthcoming from nonexecutive board members could indeed come to full expression in the process of policy-making. That this is doubtful emerged from our findings that the executive management and the chief executive are considered to have much more influence than the board in determining the objectives of the corporation. Moreover, there are indications that there is a tendency among full-timers to regard their part-time partners as not possessing the necessary knowledge, experience, expertise, and involvement in the affairs of the corporation needed in order to take an equal share in the responsibilities entailed in decision-making. As a result, full-timers prefer that part-timers act in an advisory capacity and make their contributions to policy decisions in that capacity. It is difficult to tell exactly what effect this attitude has on the process of policy-making, but it certainly does not enhance the share of part-timers therein.

Turning now to examine how far the contributions actually made by part-timers are congruent with those expected, the following things do emerge. In relation to two such contributions the – "broadening of horizons" and the contributions of expertise in certain fields – our findings indicate that in Britain, where part-timers are appointed on an impartial basis, they do indeed fulfill these functions. On the other hand, in Israel, where part-timers are partly officials in the various ministries and partly representatives of the "public at large," the evidence is that they do not contribute much in the way of specialized expertise or of a broader view. In both countries, however, there is agreement among board members that part-timers fulfill an important advisory function in relation to publicly sensitive matters, and also that they contribute toward "sensitizing" the board toward matters of public interest.

It is doubtful, however, whether the contribution of part-timers in regard to the public interest transcends this latter function much. Our findings indicate that in case of a conflict of interests, the majority of part-timers do not regard the defense of the public interest as their major task, despite the fact that the custody of the public interest is a major feature in their self-role image. Most part-timers, with the exception of those holding offices in the ministries, regard themselves as representing first and foremost the interests of the corporation. Those representing the various ministries tend to identify with the interests of the government; some of them even believe that this is the best way to serve the public interest.

It follows, thus, that the expectation that part-timers will counter-balance the tendency of full-timers to disregard the public interest in favor of narrow corporate interests, is only partly fulfilled. It is interesting to note in this context that only those part-timers who represent certain outside interests, like the representatives of the various ministries in Israel, perceive themselves to be caught in a true dilemma of "double loyalty." To most of the others, being loyal to the corporation comes as natural and unquestionable.

A fourth key problem delineated in Chapter 2 relates to the premises and assumptions guiding the concerns about the impact of certain characteristics of the public enterprise on the active management of these enterprises. The premises are: (a) that a multiple and conflicting goal structure might have a negative effect on the sense of direction of the active management, and might hence impair its ability to direct the enterprise toward the accomplishment of its goals; (b) that the involvement of the controlling agencies in the decision-making process might have a negative effect on the sense of self-direction of the active management and thus impair its motivation to take responsibility, to initiate action, and to innovate; (c) that the pressures and cross-pressures to which the public enterprise is exposed might create substantial role stress among the active management.

Our role-stress analysis among the chief executives reveals that the above concerns are only partly justified and that the subject is much more complex than assumed. Thus, the findings show that the chief executives are indeed disoriented by disagreements among the board members about the objectives and mode of conduct of the enterprise; that they do indeed react with feelings of powerlessness when there are disagreements between them and the rest of the board members or when their actual authority does not match the authority they consider as essential for adequately fulfilling their roles. Yet, the findings also indicate that the existence of cross-pressures does *not* create role-stress among the chief executives, and, moreover, that in certain instances the existence of such pressures actually *diminishes* the felt role-stress among the chief executives. Similarly, in certain instances the chief executives feel less cross-pressured when board members disagree among themselves. These findings are relevant to the contentions of some researchers that a multiplicity of controlling agents might result in *more* discretion for the active management (Aharoni 1981). Our findings suggest that a diversity of *views* among the controlling agents has such an effect – and it can be easily assumed that a diversity of views is quite often associated with a multiplicity of controlling agents.

Our investigation does not allow an assessment of the relative strengths of these contradicting impacts and of their net effect on the behavior of the active management. Yet, the very existence of such contradicting forces undermines to some extent the position of those who put too much emphasis on the negative effect of certain conflictual situations on the active management of the public enterprise.

Notes

[1] Support for this thesis is found in a number of empirical studies which indicate that role differentiation is indeed a source of divergent goal orientations (Dearborn and Simon 1958; Gross et al. 1958; Zald 1963).

[2] We do not enter here into a discussion of the specific contents of such orientations – which could vary depending on the background of the board members, their ties with various groups in the community, and other factors.

[3] However, part-timers are not fully shut out from this stage of decision-making, since individual consultation with part-time members is possible in principle and is actually practised from time to time.

Chapter Ten
Different Boards for Differing Situations

Our discussion so far has focused on the existing theories about the board of directors in public enterprise. The conclusions drawn from our investigation in the previous chapter were directed to these theories. Here we wish to leave this path and bring our findings into the orbit of a new perspective, the details of which will unfold gradually as we proceed.

We wish to start with the observation that in adopting an essentially "inward looking" perspective that views the environment of the public enterprise as basically irrelevant for the questions dealt with, the prevalent theories miss some important points of reference and are mistakenly led to search for the one "best solution," where no such solution exists. The basic argument developed in this chapter is that the environment of the public enterprise should be regarded as an important frame of reference for dealing with the structure-function question of the board of directors in public enterprise.

The proposition put forth may be outlined as follows. While the dilemma of how to best reconcile the aim of economic efficiency with other aims dictated by the public interest is universal, it does not take on a uniform shape everywhere. Rather, there are significant variations in the *concrete* form of the dilemma, stemming from the fact that the environmental conditions in which public enterprises operate vary widely, as a review of the relevant literature indicates. The board of directors serving as a linking-pin between the enterprise and its environment (Pfeffer 1972; Aharoni 1986: Chap. 8), should be adapted, in its structure and function, to effectively deal with the particular decision-making and control problems emanating from the environmental conditions under which the public enterprise operates. We wish to draw general support for this thesis from the extensive literature dealing with the impact of environmental factors on the structure and function of organizations and organizational units (Emery and Trist 1965; Heydebrand 1973; Lammers and Hickson 1979; Lawrence and Lorsch 1967). The more specific support derives from the series of studies led by Pfeffer on the board of directors in various types of organizations (Pfeffer 1972, 1973, 1974). In these studies Pfeffer found that the board of directors in organizations facing different problems of environmental integration utilizes different structures and functions differently. Moreover, he found that, "Organizations that deviate more from an empirically estimated optimal board structure equation are likely to perform more poorly compared to industry standards" (Pfeffer 1972: 218).

The basic position taken here is that for an improved theory of the board of directors in public enterprise, the inward looking perspective needs to be integrated with an "outward looking" perspective that relates to the relevant environmental contingencies. The importance of integrating the two perspectives will become clearer as we proceed with our discussion.

Having outlined the contours of the basic proposition, we turn now to a closer and more detailed examination of its major components. First, the major relevant environmental variations will be specified. Second, the implications of these variations for the control dilemmas facing the public enterprise will be examined. Third, the findings of the present research will be brought into orbit and combined with certain elements from decision-making theory, to argue that different control dilemmas require a different structural solution for the board of directors in public enterprise. A number of models, based on this argument will be presented. Finally, it will be argued that the suggested perspective casts a different light on some of the existing arrangements reviewed in Chapter 3, and undermines some of the criticisms levelled against them.

The Major Relevant Environmental Variables

A review of the literature shows that the major environmental variables relevant to the issue dealt with here are as follows. First, there are significant differences in the degree to which governments chose to regard the public enterprise primarily as a commercial entity or, conversely, as an instrument for achieving various public-interest aims (Garner, 1983).[1]

Thus, for example, West Germany could serve as a good example for the view that the public enterprise is first and foremost a commercial entity. The philosophy is reflected well in the following statement:

Industrial enterprises in the Federal Government find themselves, in our economic system, in competition with other enterprises, both German and foreign.

They must therefore like their competitors be managed on commercial principles. These give absolute priority to the maximization of profits.... This policy of gearing Federal shareholding to the principles of private economy has proven itself in practice. That is why it is for us the main instrument of direction. We refrain deliberately from impairing the freedom of decision of the enterprises so that the directing boards shall have the full responsibility for the results of the enterprises' activities (Garner, citing E. Pieper, West German Ministry of Finance, 1983: 10).

In Britain, however, there is less inclination "to refrain deliberately from impairing the freedom of decision of the enterprises" as is evident from the following statement:

The Government must be concerned in the strategies, and operating decisions of *public importance* [emphasis mine, M. D.] of industries which are basic to the national economy; in seeing that these industries ... are efficient; and in ensuring that there is an acceptable return on the capital invested in them (White Paper 1978: par. 3).

Many of the developing countries exemplify well an extreme opposite to that of West Germany: There the public interest issue takes precedence over the commercial issue. The reasons are manifold (Ghai 1983): Most developing countries place a much heavier reliance on public enterprises to develop and change the economy than the Western countries do. In some countries which desire simultaneously to move towards some social-ist system, public enterprises are also viewed as major means for changing the fundamentals of the economy and property relations. As a result:

The government's stake in the public sector becomes enormous, and acts as an incentive towards increasing intervention uninhibited often by political considera-tions due to the dominance of a single party (Ghai 1983: 186).

Moreover,

Since the market mechanism in many developing countries is little developed, the forms of control are often direct ... Public enterprises offer the prospect of a more direct form of control (Ghai 1983: 186).

Under such conditions, says Ghai:

A different approach to the problem of public sector autonomy than in Europe is required. While efficiency is always an important goal, it may be argued that the order of priorities ... requires primacy for policy. When important national goals are at stake, inefficiency, it may be argued, is a price one may have to pay for getting developments off the ground (Ghai: 186).

A second set of contingent factors causing variances in the autonomy-control dilemma have been termed by Anastassopoulos (1981) as "ra-tional factors." First among these is the degree to which the enterprise is exposed to market competition. Where such competition is intensive, the severe constraints imposed on the enterprise by the "invisible hand of the market" leave little room for the imposition of additional (externally) government-generated controls. Conversely, a monopolistic or quasi-monopolistic situation where the market forces are weak, leaves more scope for the exercise of choice guided by external government-imposed controls. A second factor is the extent to which the enterprise is engaged in activities which have a "public service" character, i e , activities directed at the "general interest of all citizens," as opposed to a specific group of beneficiaries. The more public the activities, the greater the scope for value judgments defining the public-interest and for external constraints enforcing the implementation of certain values.

Different Environmental Contingencies Pose Different Control Problems for the Public Enterprise

The environmental conditions discussed above have different implications for the control of public enterprise. Thus, where there is a clear political preference for economic efficiency and for a commercial orientation of the public enterprise, the major problem of control is how to ensure commercial success. Under the same political conditions, but where a monopolistic or quasi-monopolistic situation prevails, the major problem of control is how to ensure the effective use of organizational resources and how to prevent the pursuit of selfish goals and the accumulation of organizational slack through the exploitation of the environment. Similarly, where economic efficiency is still the basic aim but where, in addition, a "public service" situation prevails the major problem of control is how to ensure, besides economic efficiency, an adequate level of consumer services. Finally, where there is a clear political preference for the use of the public enterprise as an instrument for achieving a variety of political[2] goals within the economic sphere, the major problem of control is how to ensure the achievement of such goals and at the same time provide the conditions for a reasonable level of economic efficiency.

Different Control Problems Require Different Structural Solutions for the Board of Directors in Public Enterprise

If the problems of control in public enterprise do indeed vary according to varying environmental conditions, what type of board of directors, in terms of structure and mode of operation, would be best suited to deal with each of them? In seeking to answer this question we wish to relate to the findings of the present research and to certain propositions derived from decision-making theory.

The findings of the present research suggest that different structural solutions, in terms of membership composition, are required for the different control problems. This conclusion is based on the findings showing that the full-time board members, those bearing day-to-day executive responsibilities, are mostly oriented toward profitability and commercial efficiency and toward the well-being of the corporation and find it difficult to identify with other goals of public interest. The major implication of this finding is that all control situations discussed above, except for the one in which there is clear preference for a strict commercial orientation coupled with conditions of market competition, require the introduction, to the board, of *outside* members able to represent the relevant "public interest" aspects. This assertion brings us to the second set of considerations derived from decision-making theory, especially that part of it dealing with the structural and procedural solutions that are best suited for certain decision situations (Thompson and Tuden 1959; Simon 1960; Shull et al. 1970). A major relevant distinction made in this literature is between situations in which there is basic agreement on goals and the major decision problems center around finding the best means for achieving these goals, and situations in which no such basic agreement about goals exists and in which a definition of goals is part of the decision process. The proposition is made in the pertinent literature that these different decision situations require different role definitions and different procedural solutions for an effective functioning of the decision unit. In the first case, where there is basic agreement over goals and the problem is one of finding the best means for achieving them (henceforth, Type I situation), the prominent role of decision-makers is that of "expert." The major procedural avenue for reaching consensus should be through a process of mutual persuasion; voting should play only a marginal role, if at all.

In the second case, where an agreement over goals is problematic and becomes part of the decision process (henceforth, Type II situation), the prominent role of decision-makers is that of "representative." The major procedural avenue for reaching agreement should be a process of formal voting; mutual persuasion is not ruled out but cannot be expected to fulfill a leading role.[3]

The implication of the above distinctions for the question at hand is that boards requiring an introduction of outside members to represent the public interest should function differently, in terms of membership role definitions and procedures for reaching agreement, from boards composed solely of full-time members bearing executive responsibilities. The general proposition is that a board composed solely of full-timers bearing executive responsibilities should be modeled along the lines suited for Type I situations, while a board composed partly of outside members should be modeled along the lines suited for a Type II situation. We wish now to take a closer look at the different control situations delineated and analyse the board structure-function question in more precise terms.

An Outline of Some Basic Models

Commercial Efficiency as the Major Control Problem

When the major issue at stake is to ensure commercial efficiency under conditions of market competition, a board composed of mostly full-timers possessing the necessary managerial expertise seems most suitable. Broadly speaking, goal consensus is unproblematic in this situation and what is required is a body possessing the necessary expertise for ensuring the effective achievement of these goals. Since there is no real problem of representation and since the basic problem is essentially one of expert judgment, formal procedures can be built on open communication, and on consensus based on a process of mutual persuasion.

Commercial Efficiency Coupled with a Monopolistic or Public Service Situation

Where a monopolistic or public service situation requires the introduction of outside representatives on the board, to take care of the public-interest issues emanating from these situations, several requirements must be met for an effective functioning of the board. These relate partly to the mode of functioning of the board and its basic procedural framework, and partly to the selection criteria and mode of appointment of the outside members. As to the first set of requirements relating to the mode of functioning of the board, it has already been emphasized that the membership roles need to be defined as those of "representative" rather than "expert" and that voting, rather than mutual persuasion, must be the major means for reaching consensus. These provisions are necessary because, as we argued, by definition, outside members represent an orientation and interests different from those of the "expert" full-timers. Open communication and mutual persuasion are hence not well-suited for this situation. Rather, special formal procedures are required that will allow the adequate representation of all interests and that will allow an orderly process of conflict resolution.

Defining members' roles as representatives and instituting voting as the primary and basic procedure for reaching agreement and for conflict resolution, while concomitantly de-emphasizing the importance of harmony and "broad consensus" will achieve a better balance between the contributions of outsiders and insiders than the customary approach stressing the expertise inputs of members, a harmonious relationship between them, and action in the "best interests of the corporation." The institutional environment suggested above will supply the outside members, who, as we have seen, are often pushed into a marginal position by their colleagues' sense of superiority or their own insecurity as to their own skills, knowledge and proper role, with the psychological and institutional props essential for adequately fulfilling their roles: Defining their roles as representatives (rather than experts) will free them from the image of being less knowledgeable, less experienced and less expert than their full-time colleagues. Giving their specific views a legitimate outlet in voting procedures, rather than exposing them to the suffocating climate of "broad consensus" and "harmony" will instill in them a sense of power, self-confidence, and independence. The "voice" with which they are equipped will thus become a real input in the decision process, rather than a faint echo of their colleagues'. Obviously, the voting procedures introduced must be designed to achieve the desired balance of interests, and this is a subject which requires special attention on the part of decision-makers, deciding on the nature of the institutional framework of the board of directors in public enterprise.

Special attention also needs to be given to procedures that will ensure an adequate supply of information to outsiders. As our and other researches show, adequate information is a major problem in the case of outsiders since they have no direct access to "inside" information and since full-timers are reluctant to provide full information. This means that special procedural provisions are necessary to ensure that outsiders get the information necessary for adequately fulfilling their representative role.[4]

As to the mode of appointment and selection criteria applied to outside members, there are the following basic requirements. These members should be appointed on a part-time basis, should possess the necessary judgmental capacities for adequately fulfilling their roles, and should have a clear sense of their role and mission. The requirement of judgmental capacities commensurate to the role to be filled is obvious and needs hardly any elaboration. Yet the other requirements need some explanation: A part-time appointment is necessary to lessen the organizational involvement of the members so appointed and to prevent their self-interest in the company's welfare from influencing their decisions. A clear role definition is needed since it is a sine qua non for effective role fulfillment, and much more so when the role is representational. In the latter case, where conflict is almost unavoidable, representatives need to know very clearly what their mission is and what they are representing. Our research findings showing that many part-timers suffer from a lack of a sense of what their "true" mission is because of the diffuseness of the "public interest" concept, indicate the need for a more tangible anchorage point for defining their role. A specification of the major control problems facing the public enterprise operating under certain environmental conditions can greatly assist in this task since a "narrower" and more precise definition of the public interest can be derived through it. Similarly, our research findings showing that part-timers fail quite often to enact their role as representatives of the public interest and tend to identify with "the corporation" indicate the need for a better-defined role. A role definition that stresses the representative aspect of their roles and defines more clearly the subject and area of representation should provide the psychological and institutional support necessary for effectively fulfilling that role. The major variations within the framework of the general conditions specified above would concern part-time membership recruitment and selection criteria as well as the role definitions of the part-timers. Thus, in a monopolistic or quasimonopolistic situation, where the major function of part-timers is to ensure the efficient use of organizational resources and to prevent the accumulation of organizational slack through an exploitation of the environment, the major part-time membership selection criterion should be the possession of an expertise which will enable effective discharge of functions, i. e., managerial experience and knowledge directly relevant to the enterprise's field of operation. The role definition of part-timers should explicitly refer to their function as "watchdogs" as defined above.

In a similar vein, in a public-service situation where the major control problem is to ensure adequate services to the consumers, the major selection criterion applied to part-time members should be their ability to adequately represent the consumers' needs and define effectively these needs in terms of such questions as service availability, service quality and reliability, service timeliness and convenience, and questions of pricing. Their role should be clearly defined as one of consumer representatives. The task of finding the right candidates is, to be sure, not an easy one and is fraught with many problems (e. g., Tivey 1982) – yet it is not completely insurmountable.

To prevent or at least lessen informal intervention by the responsible minister and his officials, in the above-defined situations, appointments to the board could be disassociated from ministerial patronage which has been severely criticized on the grounds that:

Statutes authorizing appointments usually provide no guidance, merely allocating the power to the minister. . . . each appointment is an executive action for which no explanation or justification must be offered to parliament or the public. . . . in practice many appointments are effectively made by departmental officials with only formal ministerial approval (Davies 1982: 171).

The result is that many are of the "ever-adaptable amateur 'all-rounder'" variety (1982: 169) and it is easy for the executive to use the system "as a means for reward or appeasement for 'baronial henchmen'" (1982: 179).

A detailed discussion of alternatives for, and/or reform in ministerial patronage of appointments and their advantages may be found in Davies (1982). They include: opening up the nomination system, including advertising, reallocation of appointment power, and the establishment of a public service commission to conduct an open and systematic process of nomination or actual appointment.

A more rational and less personal appointment system will not only lessen the dangers of informal ministerial control but, coupled with a clear definition of the tasks and with a selection process based on skill and knowledge requirements, would also lead to a part-time membership group that is much better suited to fulfill its role as representatives of the public interest.

Commercial Efficiency Coupled with a Variety of Political Goals

Where the main control problem is one of providing the conditions for using the public enterprise as a means for achieving a variety of political goals and at the same time ensure a minimum level of economic efficiency, two basic solutions present themselves. One solution is to "externalize" the political goals factor, i. e., impose the controls necessary for the achievement of the political goals externally and not through the board membership (e.g., through specific directives). In this case the board should be structured and function along the lines discussed above.

An externalization of political controls has some important advantages. One such advantage is that it contributes toward making political intentions public and leaves less room for a diffuseness of such goals. This is important for alleviating some of the conditions that undermine the sense of autonomy and self-direction among those responsible for the day-to-day conduct of the public enterprise: As our research shows, full-time board members are willing to accept a situation where the enterprise is used as a means to implement various political goals, but they find it difficult to adjust to ad-hoc intervention, to a diffuseness of objectives, and to a constant shift in objectives. An externalization of controls could contribute toward achieving a mode of control which is acceptable to the board members. Another advantage is that attempts at informal intervention would be less effective when the board is largely composed of professional full-timers, who have a strong commercial orientation and of part-timers with relatively narrowly defined "missions," since such a composition is more likely to transform the board into a rather effective "buffer" against such intervention. The ways in which external controls can be imposed are manifold and fall outside the scope of this discussion. A brief list of major mechanisms was presented in the Introduction.

An externalization of political controls seems more suitable in developed mixed-economies where a tradition of a certain amount of macro-economic planning prevails and where the institutions to carry it out exist, where political institutions are relatively well-developed and stable, and where, to paraphrase Ghai, the governments' stake in the public sector is not so enormous. Indeed, most attempts to externalize the political control function were made, with varying degrees of success, in the developed countries. Yet our review of the British and other cases shows how difficult this is to achieve, how strong the pressures are, there, and almost everywhere, for direct political control.

Where an externalization of political controls is not a viable solution, and where the conditions for an externalization of political controls do not exist, like in many developing countries where public enterprises "operate with random and limited objectives ... or with no publicly set objectives at all" (Ramanadham 1984: 112), the solution must lie within the scope of a Type II, representative, model. The basic outlines of such a model have been discussed and a repetition seems redundant. However, some specific aspects need to be emphasized. One such aspect is that government representatives, chosen on the basis of a departmental affiliation, tend to view themselves as representatives of the department with which they are affiliated and find it difficult to adopt a more "global" view, as the present research findings indicate. This means inevitably that a structure based on a departmental representation of governmental interests will function as a multiple-interest structure rather than as a dual-interest structure, like in the models presented above. An aspect related to this is that the full-time membership might find themselves as "captives" of the government representatives who hold in their hands powers not possessed by other types of public-interest representatives, such as the "power of purse" and the "power of regulation and legislation." Voting procedures need hence to take into account these special circumstances; how to balance the commercial interest as represented by the full-timers against the political interests represented by the part-timers, and how to balance the various interests of the political representatives. In addition, special attention needs to be paid to conflict-resolution mechanisms. For example, the chairman's position should be occupied by a person possessing the standing and skills that will allow him to effectively deal with the conflicts among the various government representatives.

A More Complex Structure of Control Goals

The models presented above are based on a simplifiction of situations. In actual practice the control issues facing public enterprises are quite often more complex: Quite often, a monopolistic or quasi-monopolistic situation combines with a public service situation. An even more complex situation arises when, as is often the case, the above two situations combine with a situation where public enterprises are viewed as a means for achieving a variety of political goals. These more complex situations can be dealt with by applying the principles outlined in relation to the basic models presented. For example, where a monopolistic situation combines with a public service situation, the part-time membership should be composed so as to reflect both control problems, and so forth.

The Contingency Perspective and Existing Organizational Patterns

The proposed perspective casts a different light on some of the patterns found in various countries. It is obvious that some of these do seem much more in place and much less deviant when viewed through this perspective than when viewed through the "one best solution" framework. For example, where, like in many of the developing countries, the political elite finds it difficult to formulate coherent and relatively stable goals, and has, in addition, a very high stake in the public enterprise sector, a board composed mostly of government officials does not seem to be such a bad solution – as much of the literature would like us to believe. In this case, a board composed mostly of government officials who can: "reflect the government's viewpoints in various board decisions and provide a channel of communication between the enterprise and the government" (Narain 1982: 99) seems more adequate than a wholly "neutral" board. Similarly, where the outside membership comes largely from among the representatives of various ministries, appointing as chairman a person who can deal effectively with conflicts arising between the various representatives, such as the secretary of the responsible ministry or another similarly authoritative person, seems more appropriate than appointing an impartial chairman. Only the former will have the authority, skills, knowledge, and political standing necessary to act as arbiter and final judge between the parties involved.

In a similar vein, some characteristics of the boards composed of government representatives seem less problematic when viewed through the perspective proposed here. Thus, the sometimes relatively high turnover rate of the government representatives on the board seems less disturbing when consideration is given to the fact that their major function is to bring into the decision process those values and decision-criteria that reflect the sociopolitical aims of the government, rather than contribute their expertise to the commercial operation of the enterprise. Similarly, some problems pointed out in the literature may cease to look as such when viewed through the contingency approach proposed here. Thus, a representative board, by its very nature, implies a tradeoff between sociopolitical goals and commercial goals. Complaints about the price paid, in terms of profitability/economic efficiency/commercial success, by enterprises headed by boards composed of the representatives of various ministries and interest groups seem somewhat misplaced, since the price paid is part of the tradeoff. A representative board also implies an endemic conflict of interests. A view of such conflicts as dysfunctional and an attempt to suppress them or ignore them is inappropriate; rather, conflicts should be recognized as part and parcel of the decision situation and ways should be sought for letting the various interests influence the decision process in an orderly manner. Indeed, a failure to recognize such situations for what they are and make the necessary provisions to deal with them, could prove dysfunctional. For example, a climate on the board guided by the widespread conception that harmony and avoidance of conflict are essential for the effective functioning of the board may undermine the ability of outside members to fulfill adequately their roles as representatives of the public interest: Such a climate may result in a situation where "internal conflict is minimized at the expense of the taxpayer or consumer." Similarly, the failure to pay adequate attention to the need to provide for procedures that would ensure an adequate information supply to outside members may result in a situation where these members are reluctant to express their opinion and can be "easily intimidated" as a result of not being properly informed.

The perspective proposed also sharpens our understanding of certain features of existing boards and gives us the means for evaluating their positive or negative contribution. For example, appointing to the position of chief executive in public enterprise individuals with administrative experience in various nonbusiness institutions, as is done in some of the developing countries, rather than individuals with appropriate managerial experience, obviously fulfills the function of smoothing out relationships, of lowering the propensity for conflict among the top-level decision-makers, and of making easier the acceptance of directives flowing from government and its representatives. This is also the case when the appointment of outside board members is from among retired civil servants or from among the politicians in such countries. These arrangements have been severely criticized as we have seen. We, however, wish to argue that if the purpose of these arrangements is to deliberately subvert the economic-commercial objectives to the sociopolitical aims, this is obviously a political decision with which there is little sense to quarrel. Only if this is not the case is there room for criticizing these arrangements. Only if these arrangements reflect the very widespread perception that the top-level decision-making process needs to be based on as much harmony and unanimity as possible – and its corollary that conflict and divergent interests are disruptive and harmful, and do not allow for an "orderly" decision-making process – is there room for criticism. Then our argument for a decision-making structure and process based on the recognition and legitimation of a conflict of interests, and intended to achieve some balance between sociopolitical and commercial goals, rather than subvert the one to the other, becomes directly relevant for suggesting an alternative.

Finally, the perspective proposed here also contributes toward a better understanding of some of the problems arising in certain cases. It seems that some such problems are rooted in certain incompatibilities between the prevalent institutionalized forms of the board of directors and the prevalent sociopolitical environment. For example, in Britain the numerous complaints from board members and board chairmen about "undue" ministerial intervention seem to result from an incompatibility, that has arisen over time, between a sociopolitical environment in which the dominant view is that the government "must be concerned in the strategies and operating decisions of public importance" and in which ministers tend to regard "everything as being of public importance," and a board leaning on institutional provisions basically intended to isolate it from ministerial "intervention" and whose members (well-aware of the roots of prevalent institutional provisions) "seem to believe it to be at least part of their duty to run their undertakings as successful business concerns" (Coombes 1971: 152). Indeed the NEDO (1976) report recognized this incompatibility and recommended some changes intended to alleviate it (Robson 1977). The British government rejected the NEDO recommendation for policy councils because the government, council, and enterprise "could all be concerned with strategic and major issues, and instead of clarifying responsibilities and streamlining decisions, the NEDO proposals would add an additional layer of authority, expressed in legislation, in a Policy Council whose own responsibilities would in practice have unclear demarcation lines" (White Paper 1978). Yet in practice, a modus vivendi of a different kind seems to have been found: in some instances, the right of the government to take part in the "inside" decision-making process of the public enterprise has been given formal recognition by appointing government officials to the boards.

Summary and Conclusions

The argument was put forth that the approach to the structure/function question of the board of directors in public enterprise needs to be changed. Instead of looking for the "one best solution," the environmental conditions under which the public enterprise operates should be analyzed, and a structural and procedural solution suitable for these conditions should be devised. The argument was based on the thesis that the environments under which public enterprises operate vary significantly, that these different environments pose different control problems, and that these different control problems require different structural and procedural solutions for the board of directors in order to be dealt with effectively.

A basic distinction was made between a situation where goals are agreed upon and where the major task is one of finding suitable ways for implementing them and a situation where goals are problematic and must be agreed upon as part of the decision process. The need for the above distinction arose out of a major finding of the present research showing that those charged with day-to-day executive responsibilities are basically oriented toward commercial goals and toward the well-being of the enterprise and cannot, in essence, be expected to represent the "public interest" where such interest is not entirely commensurable with the above orientation. A major implication of the above finding is that all situations that require an introduction, into the decision-making process, of public-interest goals and of values that diverge from commercial goals must be matched by a representative structure whereby the public interest is represented by others not carrying day-to-day executive responsibilities.

It was argued that each of the two basic situations distinguished above requires a different structural and procedural solution. The "expertise" type of solution, where members' roles are defined as those of experts who act on an open-communication basis, and who reach their decisions by consensus, suits the first situation where goal-consensus prevails. The "representative" type of solution where members' roles are defined as those of representatives with divergent value orientations, who act within a well-defined procedural framework and reach their decisions through a procedure of voting, suits the second situation where goals are problematic and need to be agreed upon as part of the policy formation process.

The above proposition makes it clear that a different approach is required for the board of directors in public enterprise than that derived from the typical private sector model which has as its ideal a borad whose members act in harmony, holding before their eyes "the best interests of the corporation," and who are able to arrive at a "broad consensus" through a process of mutual persuasion. Only in a situation where the sole aim is commercial efficiency and the public interest does not need to be represented by outside members, can the board be structured along the above lines. All other situations require an entirely different approach.

Two additional considerations led, in combination, to some further distinctions presented in the form of a number of basic models for the board of directors in public enterprise. One such consideration is the finding in the present research that outside directors, i. e., directors not engaged in the day-to-day management of the enterprise, and appointed to represent the public interest, find it difficult to define for themselves what the concrete contents of their roles and missions are. Such a situation, it was argued, calls for a remedy, since a lack of clarity in the definition of roles and missions might severely impair the effectiveness of role fulfillment. The second consideration is immediately relevant to the quest for such a remedy. This consideration relates to the observation that the control problems facing public enterprises differ according to the differing environmental conditions under which they operate and that an examination of these conditions enables a much clearer and much more specific definition of the public interest. Where the public interest can be specified in more definite and clearer terms the roles, missions, skill and knowledge requirements of those who are supposed to represent it can also be better defined.

The models presented are, in themselves, not entirely new: there are substantial similarities, especially in the structural-membership aspects, with some of the models encountered in reviewing the debate about the structure/function of the board of directors in public enterprise. Yet the present approach is based on a whole new set of considerations and leads to very different conclusions as to what the appropriate solutions should be. The considerations brought into focus are:

– The need to examine the environmental conditions, political, social, and economic, under which the public enterprise operates
– The need to pinpoint the control problems emanating from the various environmental conditions
– The need to take into account the basic orientations and role perceptions of the potential candidates for the board of directors, as they are reflected in empirical research, in considering the membership composition and membership selection criteria employed
– The need to institute procedures for reaching consensus, and for supplying and monitoring information flows commensurate with the membership composition and with the basic decisional situation faced by the board

The above considerations lead to a frame of thought where choices are made from a multiple-model pool with the aim of selecting the one model best suited for the particular contingencies presenting themselves[5]. This is meant on both the individual-enterprise level as well as the more global countrywide level. While the approach proposed attaches substantial weight to the sociopolitical and ideological climate prevalent in each country, it does not by any means imply a uniform solution for all the public enterprises in each country. Rather, it suggests that there is a need to consider the particular circumstances of each individual enterprise, and find a solution that fits these circumstances. In this respect the present proposal argues for a much less centralized and uniform approach to the question than is generally customary. While it is easy to understand from a political-process perspective why a "blanket" approach is appealing to the political authorities struggling with the problem of defining the managing framework of the public enterprise, we argue that it is not justified in view of the great variations in the nature of the public enterprises and their specific environments.

Notes

[1] We will not take up here the question of why these differences exist, but just mention that they reflect different historical heritages, different sociocultural conditions, different stages of socioeconomic development, and different outlooks of the dominant political elite.

[2] Here political is meant in the broadest sense of the word, rather than the narrow tactical aims of a political faction.

[3] Shull et al. (1970), for example, distinguish between three types of decision situations: routine, creative, and negotiated. Each type, according to them, requires a different strategy in terms of group structure, group roles, group process, group style, and group norms. The creative decision situation is one in which the major problem is one of finding ways and means for implementing agreed upon goals, where no clear and agreed upon solutions exist. The strategy for such a situation, which in our view describes quite well the policy formation task of the board of directors under conditions of well-defined and compatible goals, is described as follows (Shull 1970: 159–160):

1. Group structure: The group is composed of heterogeneous, generally competent personnel, who bring to bear on the problem diverse frames of reference, representing channels to each relevant body of knowledge (including contact with outside resource personnel bringing to bear on the problem expertise not encompassed by the organization), with a leader who facilitates creative or heuristic processes.

2. Group roles: Behavior is characterized by each individual exploring with the entire group all ideas, no matter how intuitively and roughly formed, which bear on the problem.

3. Group processes: The problem-solving process is characterized by
   (a) Spontaneous communication between members, that is, not focused in the leader
   (b) Full participation by each member
   (c) Separation of problem definition from generation of solution strategies
   (d) Shifting of roles, so that interaction which mediates problem-solving, particularly search activities and clarification by means of constant communication directed to both individual members and the whole group, is not the sole responsibility of the leader

(e) Suspension of judgment so that emphasis is on analysis and exploration rather than on early solution commitment
4. Group style: The social-emotional tone of the group is characterized by
  (a) A relaxed nonstressful environment
  (b) Open give-and-take between members
  (c) Interest in the problem rather than concern with short-run payoff
  (d) Absence of penalties attached to any espoused idea or position
5. Group norms:
  (a) Are supportive of originality
  (b) Seek behavior which separates source from content in evaluating information and ideas
  (c) Stress a nonauthoritarian view and independence of judgement
  (d) Are an undisciplined exploration of viewpoints
  (e) Seek openness in communication
  (f) Deliberately avoid credence to short-run results
  (g) Seek consensus, but accept majority rule when consensus is unobtainable

The negotiated decision situation is one in which "because of differences in norms, values, or vested interests" there is no agreement concerning "either ends or means or both." The authors note that here they assume a position different from Thompson and Tuden (1959), who posit that "compromise" decision-making is predicated on disagreements about ends. The strategy for such a situation is described as follows (1959: 162–163):

1. Group structure: The group is composed of proportional representation of each faction, with an impartial formal chairman
2. Group roles: Each individual conceives of himself as a representative of his faction, seeking to articulate and protect dominant concerns of the group he represents, while at the same time negotiating for an acceptable compromise solution
3. Group processes: The problem-solving process is characterized by
  (a) Orderly communication mediated by the chairman, providing opportunity for each faction to speak, but avoiding factional domination
  (b) Formalized procedures providing for an orderly handling of disputation
  (c) Formalized voting procedures
  (d) Possession of veto power by each faction
  (e) Analytical approaches to seeking compromise, rather than mere reliance on power attempts
4. Group style: Group style is characterized by
  (a) Frankness and candor in presenting opposing viewpoints
  (b) Acceptance of due process in seeking resolution to conflicts
  (c) Openness in rethinking and to mediation attempts
  (d) Avoidance of emotional hostility and aggression
5. Group norms: Group norms are characterized by
  (a) Desire on the part of all factions to reach agreement
  (b) The perception of conflict and disagreement as healthy and natural, rather than pathological
  (c) Acceptance of individual freedom and group freedom to disagree
  (d) Openness to new analytical approaches in seeking acceptable compromise
  (e) Acceptance of the necessity for partial agreement as an acceptable, legitimate, and realistic basis for decision-making

[4] A discussion about the exact procedural provisions is beyond the scope of this essay. Some proposals about voting procedures in public enterprise may be found in Raiffa (1982). A detailed discussion about the importance of information to outside members and of provisions for supplying it may be found in Waldo (1985).

[5] It is interesting to note that in a recent article that came to my attention while this book was already in press, Menon and Umpathy (1987), come to the same conclusion, namely, that control systems in public enterprise should not be uniform. The article focuses specifically on performance evaluation. A fourfold typology of control schemes is proposed based on two dichotomous dimensions: "degree of difficulty in output measurement" and "degree of complexity of organizational objectives." The role, mode of functioning and composition of the board of directors in the control schemes proposed are briefly discussed. In some respects the views concerning the board of directors fall in line with mine, but in other crucial respects there are rather sharp contrasts.

Regretfully, under the circumstances, I cannot go beyond the above remarks and discuss in greater detail the article and its proposals.

Appendix A
Corporations included in the sample

Israel

Arad Chemical Industries Ltd.
Beth-Shean Nazareth Textile
Works Ltd.
Chemicals and Phosphates Ltd.
Dead Sea Works Ltd.
El-Al Airlines Ltd.
Gapim Ltd.
Israel Shipyards Ltd.
Manoei Beth-Shemesh Ltd.
Mifalei Tovala Ltd.
Rogosin Industries Ltd.
Shewach Prefabricated Housing
Ltd.
The Electro-Optical Industries Ltd.
The United Spinneries of Israel
Ltd.
Timna Copper Mines Ltd.
Zim Israel Shipping Co. Ltd.
Zim Passenger Shipping Co. Ltd.

Britain

British Airways
British Gas
British Steel
Central Electricity Generating
Board
National Bus Company
National Coal Board

Appendix B
The interview schedule

1. What are, in your opinion, the objectives of this corporation? (Open-ended question. Sample of tentative categories: Profit-making/Earning foreign exchange from exports/Saving foreign exchange by local production/Providing employment/Developing (directing) the (particular) industry)
1a. What is the order of importance of the objectives you just mentioned? (Scoring: 1, to first in importance; 2, to second in importance, etc.)
2. In your opinion, can the the above order of importance change? (Yes/No. If yes: Under what circumstances can you envisage a change; how will the order of importance change under these circumstances?)
3. What, in your opinion, is the difference between the goals of this company as a public enterprise, and the goals of a similar enterprise under private ownership?
4. In your opinion, should this corporation be used for implementing the government's policy in the following areas:
   Employment policy   (Yes/No)
   Pricing policy   (Yes/No)
   Wages policy   (Yes/No)
   Investment policy   (Yes/No)
   Any other area (detail!)
5. Should this corporation serve, among others, as an instrument for implementing the policy of the ministry(ies) in charge of it? (Yes/No)
6. In your opinion, do your views agree with those of your superiors in regard to the following matters:
   a. The objectives of this corporation?
      (Yes/No. If no, explain)
   b. The order of importance of the corporation's objectives?
      (Yes/No. If no, explain)
   c. Whether this corporation should serve as an instrument for imple-

menting the government's policy?

(Yes/No. If no, explain)

7. In your opinion, is the existence of this corporation justified without profitability?

(Yes/No. If yes, explain)

8. Would you approve of an investment if:

a. It is profitable to the corporation but not to the economy?

(Yes/No)

b. It solves problems of employment but is not profitable to the economy?

(Yes/No)

c. It is profitable to the economy but not to the corporation?

(Yes/No)

9. Following are some questions presenting, each, two alternatives; please choose the alternative which best fits your view.

a. This company:

– Needs a board of directors

– Does not need a board of directors

b. The board of directors of this company should be comprised of:

– Experts who can help in managing the company

– Representatives of the owners and various interest groups

c. The board of directors of this company should function as

– A policy-making body which determines its goals and strategies

– As an advisory body which helps the general manager (?) in fulfilling his task and gives him the necessary backing

d. The board of directors in this company

– Fulfills the conditions mentioned by you in (b) above

– Does not fulfill the conditions mentioned by you in (b) above

– Fulfills the conditions mentioned by you in (c) above

– Does not fulfill the conditions mentioned by you in (c) above

10. In your opinion, who determines the goals of this company, and to what extent?

– a. The general manager (?)

(Very much/ Much/ Very little/ Almost not at all)

– b. The full-time board members

(Very much/ Much/ Very little/ Almost not at all)

– c. The representatives of the various ministries on the board

(Very much/ Much/ Very little/ Almost not at all)

– d. Other board members

(Very much/ Much/ Very little/ Almost not at all)

- e. The internal top-level executive body
  (Very much/ Much/ Very little/ Almost not at all)
- f. The minister responsible for the company
  (Very much/ Much/ Very little/ Almost not at all)
- g. Any other (detail!)

11. In your opinion, who should have the authority to decide on the following matters (Response categories: Chief executive and executive body/Board of directors/Government representatives)
    1. The overall investment level
    2. The lines of production
    3. The output level for each line of production
    4. The investment level for each line of production
    5. R & D investments (type level)
    6. The timing of investments and implementation schedules
    7. Pricing policy (Price level and supply terms)
    8. Employment policy (Number of employees and conditions of employment)
    9. Procurement policy (Choice of procurers and contractual terms)

12. In your opinion, who *should have* the authority to *approve* the following matters:
    (Response categories and list of matters as in (11) above)

13. In your opinion, who *actually has* the authority to *decide* on the following matters:
    (Response categories and list of matters as in (11) above)

14. In your opinion, who *actually has* the authority to *approve* of the following matters:
    (Response categories and list of matters as in (11) above)

15. In case of a conflict of interests between the parties determining the fate and policy of this corporation, whose interests should you represent?
    - The interest of the corporation
    - The interest of the government
    - The interest of the public
    - The interests of the part you represent
    - Any other (detail!)

Appendix C
The questionnaire for measuring role-stress (Means and standard deviations for each item)

The leading question:
"To what extent do you worry, in your job, about the following things?"
The response items:

1. The lack of clear policies and guidelines to help me in my job.
   ($\overline{X}$=2.85; S.D.=1.23)
2. I have to carry out my job under substantial and often contradicting pressures.
   ($\overline{X}$=3.28; S.D.=1.27)
3. I have sometimes to bypass a directive or to deviate from a certain policy in order to carry out my job.
   ($\overline{X}$=2.35; S.D.=1.01)
4. I have to do things which should be done differently.
   ($\overline{X}$=3.07; S.D.=1.07)
5. I am not always clear about the scope of my authority.
   ($\overline{X}$=1.50; S.D.=0.65)
6. The feeling that I do not have enough influence over the actions and decisions of my superiors concerning the corporation and myself.
   ($\overline{X}$=2.64; S.D.=1.15)
7. I work under incompatible orders and guidelines.
   ($\overline{X}$=2.36; S.D.=1.08)
8. I do not always know what is expected of me from persons (in parallel and superior positions) with whom I work.
   ($\overline{X}$=1.79; S.D.=0.89)
9. It is not clear what the scope and the areas of responsibility of my job are.
   ($\overline{X}$=1.50; S.D.=0.76)
10. I have sometimes to do things in my job that are against my best judgment and against my opinion.
    ($\overline{X}$=2.36; S.D.=1.28)

Respondents were asked to indicate in relation to each item the degree of felt anxiety using the following response categories:
Never/Rarely/Often/Almost all the time/All the time
(Scores: from 1–Never to 5–All the time)

Appendix D
Technical note on the content analysis

The method used had to fit the purpose of the analysis and the kind of documents analyzed. Consideration had to be given to the fact that the minutes did not contain an exact transcription of the participants' statements, and reported only approximately what was said during the meetings. Based on the above considerations, the *theme* and the *discussion* (held on a particular date on that theme) were chosen as recording and context units, respectively (for a detailed discussion on recording and context units see for example, Holsti 1969: 116–122).

Each participant was assigned a code number which was used throughout the whole process of content analysis. A given statement, made by one of the participants, was coded into the relevant category. If a statement was made more than once by the same participant all repetitions were disregarded.

To check the reliability of the coding and the suitability of the categories used, half of the themes analyzed were sampled and submitted to a second independent coder. A reliability test was performed by means of the formula developed by Scott (1955). In this test it was found that $r = 0.456$, which is the extent to which the coding reliability exceeds chance (1955: 323). Another test designed by Funkhouser and Parker (1968) was used to test the coding categories. In this test no systematic concentrations of disagreements between coders was found in relation to the categories used, nor in relation to particular items.

Appendix E
Method for the clustering of responses concerning the appropriate loci of decision/approval

(a) For each membership category (full-timers/part-timers), the responses relating to each of the items concerning the appropriate loci of decision/approval were cross-tabulated. For example, if there were two items and the responses relating to each of them were coded into one of three given categories, the following table would result:

Item a	Response category	1	2	3	Total
	1				
Item b	2				
	3				
	Total				

If there were three items a, b, c three cross-tabulations would be needed: a × b; b × c; a × c.

The congruent responses for each pair of items fall on the diagonal in each table. For each pair of items the total percentage of congruent answers was calculated.

(b) For each membership category two "matrices" (one for "authority to decide" and one for "authority to approve") of *total* percentages of congruent responses for each pair of items were obtained.

For example, if there were three items a, b, c, and the percentages of congruent responses for each pair of items were as follows:

Pair of Items	Response category	1	2	3	Total
a × b		28.6	4.8	23.8	57.2
a × c		42.9	2.4	21.4	66.7
b × c		40.5	2.4	19.0	61.9

The matrix would be:

Item	a	b	c
a	100.0	57.2	66.7
b	57.2	100.0	61.9
c	66.7	61.9	100.0

(c) The matrices were used for performing a linkage analysis according to a method developed by McQuitty (1957).

Appendix F
The clustering of responses on appropriate locus of decision (percentages)

Cluster	Membership category	Appropriate locus of decision		
		Executive management	Board of directors	Government and its representative
Investments	Full-timers	76.8	23.2	0.0
IIa*	Part-timers	51.2	46.0	2.8
Procurement/	Full-timers	100.0	0.0	0.0
Production IIb**	Part-timers	88.5	11.5	0.0
Employment/	Full-timers	92.9	7.1	0.0
Pricing Policy IIc***	Part-timers	62.5	36.35	1.0

* $\chi^2 = 10.1$, $0.02 < P < 0.01$;   ** $\chi^2 = 0.92$, $P = $ n. s.;   *** $\chi^2 = 2.57$, $P < 0.001$

Appendix G
The clustering of responses on appropriate locus of approval (percentages)

Cluster	Membership category	Appropriate locus of decision		
		Executive management	Board of directors	Government and its repre-sentative
Current Policy	Full-timers	69.9	28.5	1.6
IVa*	Part-timers	29.9	63.4	6.17
Investments	Full-timers	12.7	72.7	14.6
IVb**	Part-timers	13.2	64.2	22.6

* $\chi = 35.0$, $P < 0.001$;   ** $\chi^2 = 2.0$, $P = $ n. s.

Appendix H
The measurement of conflicting expectations[a]

(1) Disagreements between the CEO and the BMs (CEO:BMs) were measured by means of the following index (C):

$$C = (1/r) \sum_{i=1}^{r} (m/n) \qquad 0 < C < 1$$

(r = number of response categories; n = total number of BMs responding to the question; m = number of BMs who chose a different response category than did the CEO; $C = 0$ indicates full agreement between the CEO and the BMs; $C = 1$ indicates complete disagreement between the CEO and the BMs).

(2) Disagreements among the BMs themselves (BMs:BMs) were measured by means of the following discrepancy index (K) (see Coleman 1964: 441–444 for a detailed description):

$$K = \frac{n \log n - \Sigma n_i \log n_i}{n \log r} \qquad 0 = < K = < 1$$

(n = number of respondents; n_i = number of respondents who chose response category i; r = number of response categories).

(3) The discrepancies between the desired and actual allocation of decision-making powers were measured by means of an "index of incongruency" composed as follows: For each of the CEOs the desired locus of decision, for each issue, was compared with the actual locus of decision. Whenever the actual locus was identical with the desired locus, a score of 0 was recorded; whenever the actual locus differed from the desired locus a score of 1 was recorded. The scores thus obtained were averaged across all items. In this way, for each CEO two scores of incongruency were obtained: one relating to the authority to decide and one relating to the authority to approve.

[a] Note: The indices described above measure "objective" incongruencies in expectations, i.e., the expectations of CEOs and those of BMs are measured individually and thereafter compared with each other. One

may question the adequacy of such indices since it is possible to argue that the degree of role-stress experienced is a function of *subjectively* felt conflicts which are not necessarily identical with *objective* incongruencies in expectations. While we agree in principle with the logic of this argument, we contend that the degree of discrepancy between felt and objective incongruencies in expectations, depends on the particular circumstances in question. In our case, it may be assumed that because of the intensive interaction and high interdependencies between the CEOs and BMs, there would be no significant discrepancies between the subjective and objective incongruencies in expectations.

Appendix I
The indices of role-stress

The final indices of role-stress were obtained as follows. The responses to all the ten items in the role-stress questionnaire were analyzed by principal factoring (as in Nie et al. 1970: Chap. 17). Three principal factors were obtained which accounted for about 72% of the total variance. The first factor was labelled *anomie* since all the high loading items (except for one) indicated feelings or normlessness and powerlessness. The second factor was labelled *self-role-stress* since most of the high loading items on this factor indicated stress from having to do things with which one does not fully agree. The third factor was labelled *intersender role-stress* since most high loading items on this factor indicated feelings of stress stemming from conflicting pressures from role-partners.

From among the high loading items on each factor those were chosen which had a relatively high discriminative power and a communality of more than 0.50. The assumption was that the communality could be used as an indicator of reliability (e.g., Harman 1968: 10; Fruchter 1954: 47–49).

References

Aharoni, Y. (1970): The Workings of Boards of Directors in Israel. Report, Israeli Institute for Production and Productivity, Tel-Aviv (Hebrew).

Aharoni, Y. (1979): State-owned Enterprises in Israel and Abroad. Tel-Aviv: Gomeh (Hebrew).

Aharoni, Y. (1981): "Managerial discretion in state-owned enterprises." In: Raymond Vernon and Yair Aharoni (eds) State Owned Enterprise in the Western Economics. London, Croom Helm, 184–193.

Aharoni, Y. (1982): "State-owned enterprise: an agent without a principal." In: Leroy P. Jones (ed) Public Enterprise in the Less Developed Countries. New York: Cambridge University Press, 67–76.

Aharoni, Y. (1986): The Evolution and Management of State Owned Enterprises. Cambridge, Mass.: Ballinger.

Aharoni, Y. and Ran Lachman (1982): "Can the manager's mind be nationalized?" Organization Studies 3 (1): 33–46.

Anastassopoulos, J. P. (1981): "The French experience: conflicts with government." In: Raymond Vernon and Yair Aharoni (eds) State Owned Enterprise in Western Economics. London: Croom Helm, 99–116.

Appleby, P. M. (1956): Re-examination of India's Administrative System with Special Reference to Administration of Government's Industrial and Commercial Enterprises. New Dehli: Government of India, Cabinet Secretariat.

Baran, P. and P. M. Sweezy (1968): Monopoly Capital: An Essay on the American Economic Order. New York: Penguin.

Barker, A. (1982): Quangos in Britain. London: Macmillan.

Barnard, C. I. (1938): The Functions of the Executive. Cambridge, Mass.: Harvard University Press.

Barrett, G. V. and B. M. Bass (1970): "Comparative surveys of managerial attitudes and behavior". In: J. Boddewyn (ed) Comparative Management: Teaching, Training and Research. New York: Graduate School of Business Administration, New York University.

Baumol, W. J. (1959): Business Behavior, Value and Growth. New York: Macmillan.

Berle, A. A. (1955): The Twentieth Century Capitalist Revolution. New York: Harcourt, Brace and World.

Berle, A. A. and G. C. Means (1932): The Modern Corporation and Private Property. New York: Macmillan.

Chester, (Sir) D. N. (1952): "The Nationalized Industries." Three Banks Review (December).

Chester, (Sir) D. N. (1975): The Nationalisation of British Industry 1945–51. London: HMSO.

Child, J. (1969): British Management Thought – A Critical Analysis. London: Allen and Unwin.

Clegg, H. H. (1955): "The Fleck report." Public Administration 33.

Coleman, J. S. (1964): Introduction to Mathematical Sociology. Glencoe, Ill.: Free Press.

Coombes, D. (1972): State Enterprises: Business or Politics. London: Allen and Unwin.

Crosland, C. A. R. (1956): The Future of Socialism. London: Jonathan Cape.

Crozier, M. (1964): The Bureaucratic Phenomenon. Chicago. University of Chicago Press.

Curwen, P. J. (1986): Public Enterprises: A Modern Approach. Brighton, Sussex: Wheatsheaf Books, Harvester Press.

Cyert, R. M. and J. G. March (1963): A Behavioral Theory of the Firm. New York: Wiley.

Davies, A. (1982): "Patronage and quasi-government: some proposals for reform." In: A Barker (ed) Quangos in Britain. London: Macmillan, 167–180.

Davies, E. (1963): "Who decides the public interest?" In: M. Shanks (ed) The Lessons of Public Enterprises. London: Trinity Press.

Davis, K. and R. L. Bloomstrom (1975): Business and Society: Environment and Social Responsibility. New York: McGraw-Hill.

Dearborn, D. C. and H. Simon (1958): "Selective perception: A note on the departmental identification of executives." Sociometry 21.

Delion, A. G. (1963): Le Statut des Enterprises Publiques. Paris: Comte Editions Berger-Levrault.

Dimock, M. E. (1949): "Government corporations – A focus of policy and administration." American Political Science Review 43: 1149–1164.

Drucker, P. (1961): The Practice of Management. London: Heinemann.

Emery, F. E. and E. L. Trist (1965): "The causal texture of organizational environments." Human Relations 18: 185–209.

Escobar, J. K. (1982): "Comparing state enterprises across international boundaries: The corporation Venezolana de Guyana and the Companhia Vale do Rio Dece." In: L. P. Jones et al. (eds) Public Enterprises in Less Developed Countries, Cambridge: Cambridge University Press.

Etzioni, A. (1964): Modern Organizations. New Jersey: Prentice-Hall.

Finnegan, M. (1954): Ministerial Control of Electricite de France. Public Administration (London) Winter.

Floyd, R. H., C. S. Gray and R. P. Short (1984): Public Enterprise in Mixed Economies: Some Macroeconomic Aspects. Washington, D. C.: International Monetary Fund.

Floyd, R. H. (1984): "Topical issues concerning public enterprise." In: Floyd et al., Public Enterprise in Mixed Economies: Some Macroeconomic Aspects. Washington, D. C.: International Monetary Fund, 1–33.

Frankel, P. H. (1966): Mattei: Oil and Power Politics. London: Faber and Faber, New York: Praeger.

Fruchter, B. (1954): Introduction to Factor Analysis: Chicago: University of Chicago Press.

Funkhouser, G. R. and E. B. Parker (1968): "Analyzing Coding Reliability: The Random Systematic Error Coefficient." Public Opinion Quarterly 23: 122–128.

Garner, M. R. (1976): Relationships of Government and Public Enterprises in France, West Germany and Sweden. London: National Economic Department Office.

Garner, M. R. (1983): "The relationship between government and public enterprise." In: R. G. Reddy (ed), Government and Public Enterprise: Essays in Honor of V. V. Ramanadham. London: Frank Cass, 3–23.

Georgiou, P. (1973): "The goal paradigm and notes toward a counter paradigm." American Sociological Review 18 (3).

Ghai, Y. P. (1983): "Executive control over public enterprise in Africa." In: R. G. Reddy (ed), Government and Public Enterprise. London: Frank Cass, 181–219.

Gouldner, A. W. (1954): Patterns of Industrial Bureaucracy. Glencoe, Ill.: Free Press.

Gouldner, A. W. (1959): "Organizational analysis." In: R. K. Merton (ed), Sociology Today. New York: Basic Books, 241–270.

Graves, D. (1972): "The impact of culture upon managerial attitudes, beliefs, and behaviour in England and France." Journal of Management Studies 5: 40–56.

Gross, N. W., S. Mason and A. McEachern (1958): Explorations in Role Analysis. New York: Wiley.

Guth, W. D. and R. Tagiuri (1965): "Personal values and corporate strategy." Harvard Business Review 43: 123–132.

Haire, M., E. E. Ghiselli and L. W. Porter (1966): Managerial Thinking: An International Study. New York: Wiley.

Hanson, A. H. (1962): Managerial Problems in Public Enterprise. London: Asia Publishing House.

Hanson, A. H. (1965): Public Enterprise and Economic Development. London: Routledge and Kegan Paul.

Harman, H. H. (1968): Modern Factor Analysis. Chicago: University of Chicago Press.

Heald, D. A. (1984): "Privatization: analysing its appeal and limitations." Fiscal Studies (February).

Heald, D. A. (1985): "Will the privatization of public enterprises solve the problem of control?" Public Administration, 63: 7–22.

Heath, J. B. (1980): Management in Nationalised Industries. London: National-ised Industries Chairmen Group.

Henney, A. (1984): "Nationalized industry boards: how to make part-time members more effective?" Public Money (June) 47–50.

Heydebrand, W. V. (ed) (1973): Comparative Organizations: The Results of Empirical Research. Englewood Cliffs, N. J.: Prentice-Hall.

Hickson, D. J. et al. (1986): Top Decisions: Strategic Decision-Making in Organizations. Oxford: Basil Blackwell.

HMSO Cmnd Report 9672 (1956), par. 495–496.

Hofstede, G. (1980): Culture's Consequences: International Differences in Work-Related Values. Beverly Hills/London: Sage.

Holsti, O. R. (1969): Content Analysis for the Social Sciences and Humanities. Reading, Mass.: Addison-Wesley.

Hoover Commision Report (1949) New York: McGraw-Hill, 381–382.

Howard, J. B. (1982): "Social accountability of public enterprise: law and community controls in the new development strategies." In: L. P. Jones et al. (eds), Public Enterprise in Less Developed Countries. Cambridge, Mass.: Cambridge University Press, 77–96.

Jones, Leroy P. et al. (eds) (1982): Public Enterprise in Less Developed Countries. Cambridge, Mass.: Cambridge University Press.

Kahn, R. L., D. M. Wolfe, R. P. Quinn and J. D. Snoeck (1964): Organizational Stress: Studies in Role Conflict and Ambiguity.

Kay, J. A. and Z. A. Silberston (1984): "The new industrial policy: privatization and competition." Midland Bank Review (Spring) 8–16.

Kempner, T. A. (1974): Business and Society. London. Allen and Unwin.

Knauth, O. (1948): Managerial Enterprise: Its Growth and Methods of Operation. New York: Norton.

Lachman, R. (1985): "Public and private sector differences: CEOs' perceptions of their role environments." Academy of Management Journal 28: 671–680.

Lammers, C. J. and D. J. Hickson (eds) (1979): Organizations Alike and Unlike: International and Interinstitutional Studies in the Sociology of Organizations. London/Boston: Routledge and Kegan Paul.

Lawrence, P. R. and J. W. Lorsch (1967): "Differentiation and integration in complex organizations." Administrative Science Quarterly 17 (1).

MacMahon, A. W. (1963): Delegation and Autonomy. London: Asia Publishing House.

Maniatis, G. C. (1968): "Managerial autonomy vs. state control in public enterprises: fact and artifact." Annals of Public and Co-Operative Economy 39: 513–530.

Marris, R. L. (1964): The Economic Theory of Managerial Capitalism. New York: Macmillan.

Maurer, H. (1955): Great Enterprise: Growth and Behavior of the Big Corporation. New York: Macmillan.

McQuitty, L. L. (1957): "Elementary linkage analysis for isolating orthogonal and oblique types and typal relevancies." Education and Psychological Measurement 24 (3): 441–455.

Menon, K. and S. Umphaty (1987): "Control systems for state-owned enterprises." Annals of Public and Cooperative Economy, 58 (3): 287–304.

Merton, R. K. (1957): "The role set: problems in sociological theory." British Journal of Sociology 8: 106–120.

Mohr, L. B. (1973): "The concept of organizational goal." American Political Science Review 67: 470–481.

Monsen, R. J. and K. D. Walthers (1980): "State-owned firms: a review of the data and issues." In: Lee Preston (ed), Research in Corporate Social Performance and Policy. Greenwich, Ct., JAI Press, vol. 2: 5–156.

Morrison, H. H. (1933): Socialization and Transport. London.

Morrison, H. H. (1947): House of Commons Debate 5s ct 566 (December).

Morrison, H. H. (1954): Government and Parliament. London: Oxford University Press.

Narain, L. (ed) (1982): Autonomy of Public Enterprises. New Delhi: Scope.

NEDO (National Economic Development Office) (1976): A Study of U. K. Nationalised Industries. London: HMSO.

Nichols, T. (1969): Ownership, Control and Ideology. London: Allen and Unwin.

Nie, N. H., D. H. Bent, and C. H. Hull (1970): Statistical Package for the Social Sciences. New York: McGraw-Hill.

Nora, S. (1967): Group de Travail du Comité Interministériel des Enterprises Publiques, Rapport sur les Enterprises Publiques. Paris: La Documentation Française.

Parsons, T. (1960): Structure and Process in Modern Societies. Glencoe, Ill.: Free Press, chap. 2.

Perrow, C. (1961): "Goals in complex organizations." American Sociological Review 26 (6): 854–865.

Pfeffer, J. (1972): "Size and composition of corporate boards of directors: the organization and its environment." Administrative Science Quarterly 17: 218–228.

Pfeffer, J. (1973): "Size, composition and function of hospital boards of directors: a study of organization-environment linkage." Administrative Science Quarterly 18: 349–364.

Pfeffer, J. and G. R. Salanick (1974): "Cooptation and composition of electric utility boards of directors." Pacific Sociological Review 17: 334–363.

Phatak, A. (1969): "Governmental interference and management problems of public-sector firms." Annals of Public and Co-Operative Economy 40: 337–350.

Prakash, O. (1963): The Theory and Working of State Corporations with Special Reference to India. New York: Praeger.

Prosser, T. (1986): Nationalised Industries and Public Control: Legal, Constitutional and Political Issues. Oxford: Basil Blackwell.

Raiffa, H. (1981): "Decision Making in State Owned Enterprise". In: R. Vernon and Y. Aharoni, State Owned Enterprise in Western Economies 54–62.

Ramanadham, V. V. (1984): The Nature of Public Enterprise. London: Croom Helm.

Reddy, R. G. (ed) (1983): Government and Public Enterprise: Essays in Honor of V. V. Ramandham. London: Frank Cass.

Redwood, J. (1981): Public Enterprise in Crisis: The Future of the Nationalized Industries. Oxford: Basil Blackwell.

Redwood, J. and J. Hatch (1982). Controlling Public Industries. Oxford: Basil Blackwell.

Reith, (Lord) (1956): "Public corporations." The Times (3 July).

Rizzo, J. R. and R. J. House (1970): "Role conflict and ambiguity in complex organizations." Administrative Science Quarterly 15: 150–163.

Robson, W. A. (1962): Nationalized Industries and Public Ownership. London: Allen and Unwin.

Robson, W. A. (1967–8): Ministerial control of the nationalized industries. Report from the Select Committee on Nationalized Industries, 372-I, H. M. S. O.

Robson, W. A. (1977): "The control of nationalized industries." National Westminster Bank Quarterly 6–16.

Salter, (Sir) A. (1952): "The crux of nationalization." In: W. A. Robson (ed), Problems of Nationalized Industries. London: Allen and Unwin.

Schneyer, T. J. (1970): "Administrative responsibility in Swedish public enterprise – the problem of complex goals." Scandinavian Studies in Law 14.

Scott, W. R. (1955): "Reliability of content analysis: the case nominal coding." Public Opinion Quarterly 19: 321–325.

Seidman, H. (1970): "Government corporation: organization and control." Public Administrative Review 14.

Select Committee on Nationalized Industries (SCNIO) (1967): Ministerial Control of the Nationalized Industries, First Report, vol 1. London: HMSO.

Select Committee on Nationalized Industries (SCNIO) (1977): Reorganizing the Electricity Supply Industry, Ninth Report. London: HMSO.

Sexty, R. (1983): "The accountability dilemma in Canadian public enterprise: social versus commercial responsiveness." Annals of Public and Co-operative Economy 19–34.

Shepherd, W. G. (ed) (1976): Public Enterprise: Economic Analysis of Theory and Practice. Lexington, Mass.: Heath.

Short, R. P. (1984): "The role of public enterprise: an international comparison." In: Floyd et al., Public Enterprise in Mixed Economies. Washington, D. C.: International Monetary Fund, 110–196.

Shull, A., A. L. Delbeq and L. L. Cummings (1970): Organizational Decision Making. New York: McGraw-Hill.

Simon, H. (1960): The New Science of Management Decisions. New York: Harper.

Simon, H. (1964): "On the concept of organizational goal." Administrative Science Quarterly 9: 1–22.

Simon, H. (1976): Administrative Behavior. London: Free Press.

Stefani, G. (1981): "Control mechanisms of public enterprises." Annals of Public and Co-Operative Economy 52: 49–71.

Thompson, J. and A. Tuden (1959): "Strategies, structures and processes in organizational decision." In: J. Thompson et al., Comparative Studies in Administration. Pittsburg: University of Pittsburg Press 195–216.

Tivey, L. (1973): Nationalization in British Industry. London: Jonathan Cape.

Tivey, L. (1982): "Quasi government for consumers." In: A. Barker (ed), Quangos in Britain. London: Macmillan 137–151.

Vernon, R. (1981): "Introduction". In: R. Vernon and Y. Aharoni, State Owned Enterprise in Western Economies 54–62.

Vernon, R. and Y. Aharoni (eds) (1981): State Owned Enterprise in the Western Economies. London: Croom Helm.

Waldo, C. N. (1985): Boards of Directors: Their Changing Roles, Structures and Information Needs. Westport, Conn.: Quorum.

Warner, K. W. and A. E. Havens (1968): "Goal displacement and the intangibility of organizational goals." Administrative Science Quarterly 12: 539–555.

White Paper (1961): The Financial and Economic Obligations of the Nationalized Industries. Command 1337. London: HMSO.

White Paper (1978): The Nationalized Industries. A Review of Economic and Financial Objectives. Command 7131. London: HMSO.

Whythenshawe, (Lord) S. (1957): The Boards of Nationalized Industries. London: Longmans.

Williamson, O. E. (1967): The Economics of Discretionary Behavior. Chicago: Markham.

Zald, M. N. (1963): "Differential perception of goals." Sociological Quarterly 4 (3).

Author Index

Subject Index

in Israel 33, 38, 71. *And see* Israel, public corporations.
individual characteristics within 41
legitimating capacity of 19
models of organization 3, 40. *And see* model.
perceived actual powers of 51, 97
„politicized" 40
relationships with government 26, 51ff, 79, 95, 99, 106, 108
„right" and „wrong" choices 40
structural solution for 119, 128–129
structure 20, 24, 115–116
structure–function 21, 42, 115, 120, 128, 130
theory of 1, 5, 115
tripartite conception of 23
Brazil 8
Britain. *See* United Kingdom.
British Airways. *See* United Kingdom public corporations.
British Gas Corporation. *See* United Kingdom public corporations.
British Leyland. *See* United Kingdom public corporations.
British Steel Company. *See* United Kingdom public corporations.

Canada 8
Central Electricity Generating Board. *See* United Kingdom public companies.
CGT (Compagnie Generale Transatlantique). *See* France.
chairman of the board 22, 45, 57–58, 105, 126
Chemicals and Phosphates. *See* Israel public corporations.
chief executive officer (CEO) 3, 51, 80, 87ff, 112, 126
anomie in. *See* anomie.
areas of responsibility 91
as *tertius gaudens* 97
discretionary powers of 89, 98

disagreement with board members 88, 91ff. *And see* board members, disagreements with chief executive officers.
goal orientations of 89
role-stress in 87ff, 113–114
civil servants 36, 43, 127
cluster analysis 72ff, 142
locus of approval 145. *And see* locus of approval.
locus of decision 142–144. *And see* locus of decision.
commerce, international 7
commercial efficiency 3, 4, 24, 25, 26, 30, 53, 101, 103–106, 110, 119–120, 129
coupled with political goals 123. *And see* economic efficiency.
commercial flexibility 79
commissars 103
conflict
among board members 88
among board members and chief executives 88
areas of 95
internal 36, 126
measurement of 88
resolution 121, 125
types of 92
conflictful situations 32, 87, 88, 91, 95, 99, 114
conflicting expectations 89, 146
conflicting interests 85, 89, 95, 126–127
conflictual relationship between government and public enterprise 63ff
constraints 2, 5, 63, 65, 67, 68, 106
alternative testing 56
And see goals and constraints.
consumer representatives 123
consumers 15, 18, 23, 80, 123
content analysis 52, 56, 141
control
dilemmas 13, 116
external 8, 9, 10

de Gruyter Studies in Organization

WALTER DE GRUYTER · BERLIN · NEW YORK
Genthiner Straße 13, D-1000 Berlin 30, Phone (0 30) 2 60 05-0, Telex 1 83 027
200 Saw Mill River Road, Hawthorne, N.Y. 10532, Phone (914) 747-0110, Telex 646677